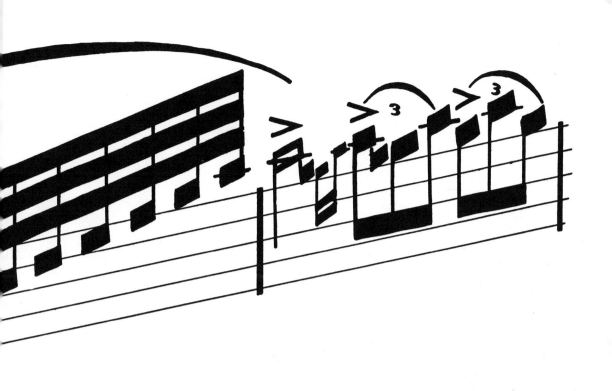

GEORGE GERSHWIN

TO IRA

★★★★EDITED AND
★★★★DESIGNED BY
MERLE ARMITAGE
1938 WITH ARTICLES BY

GERS

PAUL WHITEMAN ★ OLIN DOWNES ★ WALTER DAMROSCH
GEORGE GERSHWIN ★ MERLE ARMITAGE ★ OTTO H. KAHN
ARNOLD SCHOENBERG ★ WILLIAM DALY ★ HAROLD ARLEN
OSCAR HAMMERSTEIN II ★ ISAMU NOGUCHI ★ DAVID EWEN
NANETTE KUTNER ★ LESTER DONAHUE ★ ISAAC GOLDBERG
ERMA TAYLOR ★ GILBERT SELDES ★ J. ROSAMOND JOHNSON
RUDY VALLEE ★ LEONARD LIEBLING ★ ALEXANDER STEINERT
ALBERT HEINK SENDREY ★ JEROME KERN ★ DuBOSE HEYWARD
HENRY A. BOTKIN ★ SAM H. HARRIS ★ ROUBEN MAMOULIAN
EVA GAUTHIER ★ FERDE GROFÉ ★ LOUIS DANZ ★ TODD DUNCAN
BEVERLEY NICHOLS ★ IRVING BERLIN ★ S. N. BEHRMAN
GEORGE ANTHEIL ★ IRA GERSHWIN ★ SERGE KOUSSEVITZKY

DA CAPO PRESS • NEW YORK

GEORGE
HWIN

INTRODUCTION BY EDWARD JABLONSKI

Library of Congress Cataloging in Publication Data

George Gershwin / edited and designed by Merle Armitage; introduction by
Edward Jablonski.—1st Da Capo Press ed.
  p.   cm.
Originally published: New York: Longmans, Green & Co., 1938. With new
introd.
  ISBN 0-306-80615-0
  1. Gershwin, George, 1898–1937. I. Armitage, Merle, 1893–1975.
ML410.G288G46 1995
780′.92—dc20

94-37445
CIP
MN

First Da Capo Press edition 1995

This Da Capo Press paperback edition of *George Gershwin* is an unabridged
republication of the edition published in New York in 1938, with the
addition of a new introduction by Edward Jablonski.

Published by Da Capo Press, Inc.
A Subsidiary of Plenum Publishing Corporation
233 Spring Street, New York, N.Y. 10013

INTRODUCTION

Merle Armitage (1893-1975) was a cosmopolitan man of many parts. He began an enterprising career on his father's cattle ranch in Iowa. At eighteen he abandoned civil engineering because working in the glaring sun during the day and at a drafting board at night damaged his eyes. Besides, he had other interests.

In 1921 he published a magazine article expounding his ideas for innovative theatrical staging that led to an invitation to join the staff of an important American impresario, Charles L. Wagner. This brought him into the company of such musical luminaries as John McCormack, Mischa Elman, Mary Garden, and Paderewski, among others. Soon Armitage set out on his own as an impresario representing the likes of a French Army Band, the Scotti Opera Company (starring Geraldine Farrar), and Martha Graham.

He left New York in 1924 for Los Angeles, where he co-founded the Los Angeles Opera Association and was "appalled by the anemic, colorless art produced in the then remote and provincial Los Angeles." As for Hollywood, he was equally appalled to learn that the "whole concept of abstract art baffled its film-preoccupied natives."

He began another career, that of educator in the realm of contemporary art. (One of his earliest publications, a pamphlet containing one of his lectures, was entitled *The Aristocracy of*

Art [1929]). Among his creations over nearly three decades were volumes devoted to Picasso, Klee, Rockwell Kent, and the photographs of Edward Weston. He also designed books written by others. Included among his subjects were food, the U.S. Navy, and Pueblo pottery.

Contemporary book design affronted him. As he explained in a catalog of an exhibition of his work at the University of Texas, Austin, in 1963, "My adventure into book making had three incentives, or points of departure. It seemed to me that the design of books, all books, had fallen into a pattern. The most casual investigation of a library disclosed that books in all categories wore the same dress. Yet no producer would play Shakespeare, Gilbert and Sullivan and *South Pacific* in identical decor.

"My aim was to relate the design of the book to the subject of the text. Secondly, new creative persons were coming into public notice whose aims as artists were largely misunderstood.

"These motivations all converged into my feeling a necessity to embrace an avocation that gave a sympathetic change from my arduous duties as an impresario . . .

"Naturally, what I did stirred up violent criticism. I became, in certain circles, the destroyer of book tradition, the bad boy of typography, the usurper of placid pools of bookmaking. But through the years some of my most criticized inventions have been quietly adopted, i.e., use of the end-sheets, double-page title pages, large readable type, generous margins, etc. . . . "

These ideas were first applied when he wrote and designed his first book devoted to sculptor Maier-Krieg (published by Knopf in 1932).

He included contemporary composers among the misunderstood artists of our time. In 1936 Schirmer published his *Strawinsky*, edited by Armitage with several perceptive articles, drawings, designs, and superb photographs by Weston. It was the first book about Stravinsky published in America, and a handsome one. His next musical subject was the even more problematical Arnold Schoenberg, recently settled in Los Angeles. The resultant book was published in 1937. One of the purchasers of a signed (by Schoenberg) copy was another new resident (though in Beverly Hills), George Gershwin.

Gershwin and Armitage had met in New York in the 1920s, at the theater, concerts—and art galleries, for both had become avid collectors of art, especially that then called "modern." When he heard of the arrival of the Gershwins in California, Armitage decided to place his vocation at the composer's disposal. Early in October 1936 he suggested an All-Gershwin concert, featuring Gershwin as soloist, with the Los Angeles Philharmonic the next year. Gershwin, who was not kept especially busy by his film studio, agreed. He not only performed the solos in *Rhapsody in Blue* and the *Concerto in F*, with Alexander Smallens conducting, but also served as conductor for the *Cuban Overture* and selections from *Porgy and Bess*.

Set for February 10th and 11th, 1937, the concerts in Philharmonic Hall were sold out and, as Armitage recalled, "Hundreds were turned away for lack of seats at each performance. As a matter of fact we were sold out a week before the concerts and had to return checks for seats from all over the West."

It was during a rehearsal of the *Porgy and Bess* section and, in the evening, the performance of the *Concerto*, that Gershwin first experienced signs of the illness that would take his life. While rehearsing the chorus and orchestra, he fleetingly lost consciousness and nearly fell from the podium. He brushed away any assistance, saying he was all right and that he had merely lost his balance. During the playing of the *Concerto in F* he suffered a momentary blackout and lost his place in the piece. Smallens covered for him and soon Gershwin finished the concerto with his customary élan.

A medical checkup that followed revealed no organic disorder and Gershwin continued his work with his brother Ira on their films. Around this time he and Armitage began discussing a West Coast revival of Gershwin's "labor of love," *Porgy and Bess*, which had been a failure in New York and had closed after a brief tour. Gershwin was excited about this possibility, and he and Armitage spent a great deal of time discussing this as well as other Gershwin plans, including a string quartet that Gershwin had "written in his head," but not on paper.

Between the February incident and the final, fatal manifestation in July, Gershwin suffered other indications of illness—headaches, the smell of burning rubber, dizziness. This was attributed by many to his unhappiness in Hollywood, a diagnosis which was confirmed by a battery of physicians who could find nothing physically wrong—though there was a hint of the possibility of a brain tumor. Gershwin, however, refused to submit to a painful spinal tap which would reveal, in fact, that he had a fulminating tumor. When the attacks worsened, Gershwin spent several days in a hospital for tests and was again released. A couple of weeks later, early in July, the attacks became more severe and on July 9th he slipped into a coma; on the eleventh, following surgery for a cystic tumor of the brain, he died.

Armitage had returned from Europe that day, heard the news of Gershwin's illness, and was shocked upon calling the hospital to learn that his friend had died five minutes before. Determined to keep his promise to Gershwin, Armitage went ahead with his plans of a West Coast revival of *Porgy and Bess* in 1938.

He turned next to his avocation. "We had become great friends because of our mutual interest in music and art," Armitage wrote. "George had a fine collection of contemporary paintings, and was an accomplished painter himself. His passing was a sad moment for me. The memorial edition of *George Gershwin* was a work to which I dedicated a solid year, and persuading a group of celebrities to write was a problem in itself. In design, I aimed at infusing the book with some of the vitality, color and excitement that were manifest in this great American composer."

He succeeded, creating one of the most valuable and elegant books about Gershwin. In planning the book's content Armitage had the brilliant idea of asking for essays from often trying celebrities (some of whom did not contribute) and to reprint, and thus preserve, a dozen earlier articles about the composer, most published during his lifetime.

Of the pieces written especially for the book, Ira Gershwin's "My Brother" is outstanding—factual, informative, and objective. Rouben Mamoulian's psychological probing is fascinating in its portrait of a gifted, sometimes troubled young man. There are the expected tributes from his close friends and fellow-workers, Harold Arlen, Irving Berlin and Jerome Kern; the first and last provide small, illuminating vignettes of a man some regarded as self-centered and an egotist. Of special interest are the views of Gershwin by members of a group to which he did not belong—the conservatory-trained musicians: George Antheil (a student of Constantin von Sternberg and Ernest Bloch), Alexander Steinert (a student of Charles Martin Loeffler and Vincent d'Indy) and, of course, Arnold Schoenberg. It would be a couple of decades before others of their fraternity, most of whom approached Gershwin with condescension and envy, caught up with them in appraising—and even admiring—Gershwin and his music.

Of the reprinted pieces, the two by Gershwin himself are treasures, as is his friend William Daly's acerbic reply to an assertion that he did Gershwin's orchestration for him. There are two delightful period pieces that capture the young composer coming into his own, Beverly Nichols's snappy Jazz Age portrait and S. N. Behrman's urbane *New Yorker* "Profile." DuBose Heyward's affectionate, admiring article on Gershwin and the writing of *Porgy and Bess* should never have gone out of print.

The same can be said for this ingeniously conceived and executed book. There is simply no equal to this unique tribute to the "modern romantic" who was and forever will be the great American composer, George Gershwin.

–Edward Jablonski
September 1994
New York City

Edward Jablonski is the author of Harold Arlen: Happy with the Blues (*also available from Da Capo Press*), Gershwin, The Encyclopedia of American Music, *and many other books; he is the coauthor of* The Gershwin Years, *and edited* Gershwin Remembered. *He has lectured at Pennsylvania State University and elsewhere on Gershwin and Arlen, and has written, served as a consultant for, and appeared on several Gershwin documentaries.*

CONTENTS

CONTENTS

PREFACE

"But then even in the most insignificant details of our daily life, none of us can be said to constitute a material whole, which is identical for everyone, and need only to be turned up like a page on an account book or the record of a will; our social personality is created by the thoughts of other people . . ."

MARCEL PROUST in "Swann's Way."

This book is written by friends of George Gershwin, many of whom played important rôles in his career. Each person invited to write for this book has been given complete freedom, but encouraged to cover whatever aspects of life, work or personality of George Gershwin they knew best. Other friends and associates of George Gershwin were invited to contribute, who for reasons best known to themselves, failed to respond.

As Editor, my function, in addition to my own article, has been to correct noticeable mis-statements of fact, and to exclude matter which did not seem to be illuminating. I have not altered the style of a single writer. The impression which results from these variegated sketches is as many-sided as was the man himself. Few figures of recent times lend themselves so aptly to composite treatment as the versatile George Gershwin.

The reader will be amused to find that certain writers, in putting down their impressions of George Gershwin, are frequently presenting their self portraits. It is interesting to observe how many eminent men were unaware of Gershwin's real achievement, or obviously misunderstood it. But taken as a whole, the thirty-eight articles contained in this book cover a remarkable range of interests, and reflect a warm and glowing portrait of this extraordinary musician and man who exerted a very real influence in his art, and on his time.

M. A.

TO GEORGE GERSHWIN

Our friend wrote music
And in that mould he created
Gaiety and sweetness and beauty
And twenty-four hours after he had gone
His music filled the air

And in triumphant accents
Proclaimed to this world of men
That gaiety and sweetness and beauty
Do not die . . .
A genius differs from other men
Only in that his immortality is tangible
What he thought, what he felt, what he meant
Has been crystallized in a form of expression
A form far sturdier than the flesh and sinew of the man
But lesser beings than geniuses
Leave their marks upon this earth
And it is as a lesser being
That George Gershwin's friends knew him and loved him
We remember a young man
Who remained naïve in a sophisticated world
We remember a smile
That was nearly always on his face
A cigar
That was nearly always in his mouth
He was a lucky young man
Lucky to be so in love with the world
And lucky because the world was so in love with him
It endowed him with talent
It endowed him with character
And, rarest of all things,
It gave him a complete capacity
For enjoying all his gifts.

2

It was a standing joke with us
That George could not be dragged away from a piano
He loved to play the piano
And he played well
And he enjoyed his own playing
How glad we are now
That some divine instinct
Made him snatch every precious second
He could get at that keyboard
Made him drink exultantly
Of his joy-giving talent
Made him crowd every grain of gratification
He could get into his short, blessed life
Maybe the greatest thing he left us
Is this lesson
Maybe we take the good things of life
Too much for granted
Maybe we took George too much for granted
We loved him
Should we not have loved him more?
Have we ever loved him so much
As we do now?
Have we ever said so
As we do now?
We are all inadequate, muddling humans
With hearts and minds woefully unequipped
To solve the problems that beset us

3

We are eloquent in the recognition of our troubles
Why are we not equally eloquent
In the recognition of our blessings
As George was?
Some will want a statue erected for him
He deserves this
Some will want to endow a school of music
In his name
He deserves this
But his friends could add one more tribute:
In his honor
They could try to appreciate
And be grateful for
The good things in this world
In his honor
They could try to be kinder to one another ...
And this would be the finest monument of all.

OSCAR HAMMERSTEIN II

1938·MERLE ARMITAGE

George Gershwin was proud that he was an American. When he said, "My people are American; my time is today—music must repeat the thought and aspirations of the times"—he was giving verbal utterance to a quality his music invariably expresses. Today, pride in America can be manifest without fear of being thought either presumptuous or naïve. We are aware, now, of its scope, of its vastness. We have a new appreciation of its vitality, a new understanding of its tremendous contribution. In every way it is big. Whether natural or man-made, there is no pettiness in America's contours. The effect which this huge vision has had upon our people is one of the subtle differences between the American and the European. We may be, and sometimes are, crude and immature, but we are a big, a vital people—fortunately removed from the suspicions and rancors of more exhausted and disillusioned races. We reveal this in our manners, activities and appearances. The fact that George Gershwin was a Jew, and that many of his musical sources were Negroid confirms his basic Americanism. For this is not a country of race, it is a country of races.

The excitement, the nervousness and the movement of America were natural motivations in Gershwin's life and Gershwin's music. It is a commonplace that during his lifetime his music had little discerning critical appraisal. Admirers and friends, the thousands who had fallen in love

5

with his music, distorted judgments—crowded out the possibility and opportunity for detached, considered evaluations. And while Gershwin may not be destined for the exalted sphere which some of his more fatuous followers prophesied, his importance is immeasurably greater than has been imagined by many in High Places. And the only logical explanation of this remarkable range of evaluation is that George confused both camps, because he was unique. Reactions to the world and things within it are the result of two conditions—our natural perspicacity—added to which is growth through experience. The degree to which we may add to natural sensitiveness is in direct ratio to our mental and emotional flexibility. Because of the average inflexibility of individuals who become static and impervious to the overtones of the world, there always exists the problem of the introduction of new ideas and esthetic possibilities. Most minds do not function as thinking machines, but as cataloging machines. Most music worshippers are data and record collectors, or comparisonists of microscopic details. Seldom do they comprehend the music itself.

America had almost overcome its musical inferiority complex, through its possession of more first class symphony orchestras than could be heard in all of Europe, when its smugness suffered a slight shock. A denizen of Tin Pan Alley was first tolerated, then *invited* into the temples of great music!

Although many European critics had long since recognized the vitality of American jazz, and had written of the extreme probability that jazz and the technique of jazz would affect the constitution of the symphony orchestra and composition of the future, we were much too complacent with our foreign importations to risk admiring a home-grown

6

product, and much too un-sure of its importance—at least many of us were. We were unaware also that jazz had exerted a great influence on European art. Indeed, Negroism has from Gauguin to Modogliani, to Picasso and Derain, had many followers in painting. Debussy wrote more than one "cake-walk" even before 1914. The influence is apparent in certain early works of Strawinsky, Milhaud and Hindemith. Intellectual Europe had recognized the first convincing esthetic American development.

Quite the contrary was the situation in America. Because jazz had been quickly accepted by the masses as a natural expression, the more informed public, as well as the critics, had tabulated and abandoned it as a rhythmical expression for bestial instincts in all their primitive force, and nothing else. We have already forgotten the tumult and the shouting which existed in the early 1920's in regard to the decadence of the jazz age. Reactionaries of both continents found jazz a most satisfactory target for their invective. Case in point: In London, on October 8, 1927, Sir Henry Coward, one of England's leading musicians and a world authority on choral technique, said "a lowering of our moral standards and a consequent loss of the prestige to the white race in the world" would be among the dire results of the vogue of jazz. We had not recognized that anything vital, anything convincing, anything truly important in American art must have its roots in our own soil and our own environment. Lacking insight and awareness, we did not perceive, (to quote Louis Danz' neat sentence) that "A season with Andre Lhote might *not* make an American painter, nor a prize scholarship with Nadia Boulanger an American composer."

Into this milieu the figure of George Gershwin was projected. Already, in certain quarters, he was damned, for he had written the outrageously

7

successful *Swanee* for Al Jolson, and several of *George White's Scandals*. One of the *Scandals* so impressed Paul Whiteman, who had longed to take jazz into the concert halls, that he invited George to contribute to that certain Aeolian Hall concert on February 12, 1924, when the world first heard the *Rhapsody in Blue.* Not all the critics, of course, patronized jazz nor underrated Gershwin. Deems Taylor, for instance, wrote that Gershwin was "a link between the jazz camp and the intellectuals." But the thing which was not apparent, seemingly to anyone at the time, was that the forces behind the natural evolution of music were making use of a certain instrument—that instrument being known in the flesh as George Gershwin.

There were other American composers — living and dead. But they were imitative, not only of the methods of Europe but of its spirit, and a spirit which was and is decadent. These composers had attempted to cover their weaknesses of spurious inspiration with inventions, with external showiness which often deceived the unknowing. As a matter of fact, even today the long arm of Europe still stretches its deadening hand of tradition; still exercises its authority over many American developments, causing the true spirit of America to be submerged. To follow the MacDowells, the Parkers, the Cadmans and the Hadleys of the past and the present, who have taken over a foreign art ready-made and are imitating it with some success, but with a complete absence of vital force, *is not the future,* therefore, of the American composer. That future will be captured by the contemporary-minded American, whose awareness has apprised him of our divergence; the man who knows that ours is a different but not an inferior contribution, who has abandoned academic romanticism, and who knows that there is such a thing as the esthetic of the engineers and architects.

8

A number of highly-endowed individuals among American composers, men who were aware of trends on both sides of the Atlantic, were beginning to have an influence in American music; they were restricted, however, to a comparatively small group. Roger Sessions, George Antheil, Aaron Copland, Louis Gruenberg, and later Roy Harris, had changed the entire picture of American composition and given it a new prestige. But these men were in an impasse. They were without an audience.

Gershwin came to bat, so to speak, with the bleachers full.

When the New York Symphony Society, through Walter Damrosch, commissioned Gershwin to compose a work of symphonic proportions, it resulted in the *Concerto in F*. When, in turn, this work was heard in Carnegie Hall with Damrosch conducting and the composer at the piano, the capacity audience was synthetic—consisting of one-third curious intellectuals, one-third conservative subscribers, and one-third Gershwin devotees. Gershwin — from the time Paul Whiteman had programmed the *Rhapsody in Blue*—never was without an audience. The musical purists, however, found George in many respects inadequate. Among the more frequently heard criticisms were his inability to sustain a phrase more than sixteen or thirty-two bars long, the clumsiness of his orchestration, his ill-formed arias *(Porgy and Bess)*, and other faults in the fundamentals of structure. To use a very hackneyed but telling phrase, they were unable to see the forest for the trees. George Gershwin brought to serious consideration a new idiom in music, and forever changed its future direction.

Let us superficially investigate the anatomy of jazz. If ragtime was a homophonic horizontal music; jazz, at its boldest, is polyphonic, polyrhythmic and vertical. One authority says jazz is a compound of (a) the fox trot rhythm, a four-four measure (alla breve) with a double accent, and (b) a syncopated melody over this rhythm. However, no mere formula will make jazz. As an illustration, a highly syncopated line like the second subject in Cesar Franck's *Symphony in D Minor,* or the principal theme of Beethoven's third *Leonora* overture is merely syncopation until you add to it the heavy bump-bump of the fox trot beat. The combination, on the authority of Virgil Thomson, is jazz. It is a mistake to speak of jazz as a product of the Negro, although its primary associations such as its rhythm are black and derive ultimately from the African South. In the course of its filtration from the South to the cosmopolitan world it has undergone a metamorphosis, and in its development it has certainly been touched and influenced by the Hebrew.

There is considerable evidence of the fact that something approaching modern jazz existed six or seven hundred years ago. It was an epoch when men in music began to realize dimly what an amazing effect could be made by a number of people singing different things at the same time. Not being expert in combining different melodic strands, they experimented with a sort of catch-as-catch-can discant. The serious composers attacked the then colossal task of making two or three familiar tunes harmonize, and the result, we hazard, would not have been unfamiliar to modern ears. Nor is orchestral improvisation an invention of our age. Three hundred years ago the musicians in the orchestras of Monteverdi and Peri were expected to improvise counterpoint. They possessed this talent to such a degree that the more or less skeleton scores of these operas which have been saved could give us but an imperfect idea of how this music actually sounded in performance.

An orchestra like that of Paul Whiteman is in a sense a return, in a contemporary manner, to certain ancient conceptions of the orchestra. In the Whiteman band instruments have no privileges, as all the artists are equal and all timbres are valued alike. There are no more technical prejudices, for a trumpet equals a violin-cello, a saxophone may eclipse a violin, or a glockenspiel may be on a par with a Stradivarius. It is a magnificent collaboration where each instrument is but a tube of color at the disposal of the painter—who does not pretend that yellow is superior to blue, or that violet is more respectable than green.

The advent of Gershwin gave rise to a curious attitude on the part of certain people in the musical world. One school of thought held that jazz after all might contain something of value, but that only a Wagner or a Debussy of today, or, as they implied, a *real* composer, could make important use of it. Another school, of course, banned it all together. But certain influential people of discernment believed that Gershwin *was* a *real* composer—and knew that his music was well founded. There is an attitude today which has gained some credence, that the "larger" Gershwin works will not live, that only his songs and less pretentious compositions have the seed of immortality.

It seems to me that the question of immortality has been overstressed in every generation. Striving for permanence seems to be an incorrigible human necessity. It is difficult or impossible for us to accept the fact that immortality is relative. Often when confronted by great works of art, or moved by great music, we are inclined to say and believe that such things will never die. Yet immortality is probably only the symbol of some imperishable illusion, for measured in history's vast panorama the fecundity of some new phase certainly means the death of a now discarded one. It is conceivable that in past generations great music was written and great art created, of which not one fragment remains. Yet that great music and that

11

great art must have been necessary and helpful to the immediate following creators; and in this wise perhaps attained a sort of immortality. George Gershwin opened a musical door through which future composers can enter with comparative ease.

His works, both large and small, have been evaluated and will continue to be evaluated by musicologists, critics and intelligent amateurs.

Almost everyone is in agreement that certain songs and compositions such as *The Man I Love, Lady Be Good, Fascinating Rhythm, High Hat,* and *Mine* from *Let'Em Eat Cake,* are inimitable. Here must be mentioned *Of Thee I Sing,* in which George had the collaboration of his brother, Ira. *Of Thee I Sing* is unique in the American theatre. The support which George received from Ira in many of his musical projects must not be underestimated, as it was potent indeed. Division of opinion centers on the larger works. Yet there is a conviction and an inevitability about the *Rhapsody In Blue* which is unparalleled among American compositions of our time. In the *Concerto in F* are moments of great elevation; as, for example, the second theme in the first movement. There are a number of passages in the *Concerto* which are somewhat self-contained entities, yet the entire work has great freshness of spirit, and in this particular opus is some of George's best writing. *An American in Paris* seems to me one of the least interesting of the larger works—perhaps because of this writer's aversion to purely descriptive music. The *Cuban Overture (Rhumba)* is a work in which George took great delight, seeing in it a manner in which he wished to work in the future. Over all of these works there shines at performance a curiously Gershwin radiance—an "American 1938" variety of elation, longing at last fulfilled in settings of grandeur, exaltation at the moment of victory. Decidedly the music of youth.

12

Porgy and Bess demands separate consideration. In it George Gershwin moved forward and stepped back. He progressed in maturity, in largeness and unity of conception, in his ability to sustain. He adroitly avoided many of the clichés and meaningless conventions of opera. He stepped back, however, into old, out-moded forms. In *Porgy and Bess* is a promise of a future Gershwin *opera* in which he might have been able to eliminate even the aria. While its orchestration presents difficulties comparable to that imposed by Richard Strauss, and seems over complicated, it is yet more expert than any of its predecessors among Gershwin works. The score of *Porgy and Bess* brims with rhythmic vitality. Gershwin's use of well-defined choral pattern with its attendant pounding rhythm achieves a primitive intensity without actually resorting to Negro melodies or spirituals. So close are these to the cries of the black man that they seem to have a common origin. Three basic attributes recommend it as a candidate for posterity: (1) its soundness as music-drama; (2) its impeccability as "theatre"; (3) its singular qualities among all the attempts at writing an American opera.

If one wished to sum up George Gershwin as an artist, his own label could well be used. He spoke of himself as a "modern romantic." His music expresses it; his own painting exudes it; his collection of works of art confirms it. Perhaps nothing about George Gershwin is more revealing than his collection of contemporary paintings. He loved them, he understood them, he caressed them. He had great independence of judgment in his collecting. He had one of the finest Utrillos I have ever seen; yet it was not a "typical" example in the dealer's sense. His Modoglianis were superb, and he had fine examples by Derain, Rousseau, Pascin, John Carroll, a self-portrait by Gauguin, and was especially fond of his paintings by Se-

13

quiros, of which he had several. Musicians being notoriously indifferent to any other art, makes Gershwin's taste seem even more remarkable.

In his own painting, Gershwin had arrived at a proficiency wholly surprising in one whose life was so crowded with internal and external events. He was certainly eclectic as a painter, but this was strength, not weakness. Technically, he was the peer of many men who have national reputations as painters. He was in love with color, and his palette in paint closely resembled the color of his music. Juxtaposition of greens, blues, sanguines, chromes, and grays, fascinated him. He developed a very personal style of applying paint to canvas. And while there is no such distinction in his painting as there is in his music, yet it was a facet of his endowment which was developing rapidly, as witness the *Portrait of Schoenberg,* one of his more recent works.

Among his noteworthy achievements in paint are *Orchid,* 1934; *My Grandfather,* 1933; *Round House - 72nd Street,* 1929; *My Studio - Folly Beach,* 1934; *Jerome Kern,* 1937; *African Sculpture With Landscape;* and the *Self-Portraits.* In his drawings he had a sensitive, nervous line whose effects could be electrical. His portrait drawing of Henry Botkin, and his sketch of Adolph Lewisohn and *Girl Reading,* 1931, are examples of his competence. He seems to have entered the painter's world with little difficulty.   *   *   *

As a man, George Gershwin had qualities of heart and mind which were extremely ingratiating. He was entirely sincere. His ability to achieve a good bargain in a business sense resulted from his protecting his own very generous nature. He always seemed to be in balance. He had a very definite idea of his place in the world and of his importance as an artist —

14

yet he was modest. I have seen him blush at flattery. Although he often presented a somewhat cold exterior, I have known the inner warmth of his friendship. George Gershwin possessed the love of Broadway, the admiration of the motion picture industry, and the respect of the serious musical world — an unparalleled accomplishment.

He had one supreme quality, without which everything else would have availed little. He had style!

1938 · IRA GERSHWIN

My brother, born in Brooklyn, N.Y., September 26, 1898, was the second of four children of Morris and Rose Bruskin Gershwin. I was the oldest, then came George, then Arthur and last, our sister, Frances. Most of our early boyhood was spent on the lower East Side of Manhattan where my father engaged in various activities: restaurants, Russian and Turkish baths, bakeries, a cigar store and pool parlor on the 42nd Street side of what is now Grand Central Station, book-making at the Brighton Beach Race Track for three exciting but disastrous weeks. We were always moving. When my father sold a business and started another we would inevitably move to the new neighborhood. George and I once counted over twenty-five different flats and apartments we remembered having lived in during those days.

It was when we were living on Second Avenue that my mother added a piano to our home. George was about twelve at this time. No sooner had the upright been lifted through the window to the "front-room" floor than George sat down and played a popular tune of the day. I remember being particularly impressed by his left hand. I had had no idea he could play and found out that despite his roller skating activities, the kid parties he attended, the many street games he participated in (with an occasional resultant bloody nose) he had found time to experiment on a player-piano at the home of a friend on Seventh Street. Although

16

our piano was purchased with my taking lessons in mind, it was decided George might prove the brighter pupil.

His first teacher was a Miss Green. She was succeeded by a Hungarian band leader, impressively moustached, who was down on his uppers and condescended to take an occasional pupil. Composer of a *Theodore Roosevelt March*, his fancy ran to band and orchestra literature and George was studying a piano version of the *William Tell Overture* when he was brought to Charles Hambitzer, a talented pianist and composer of light music. Hambitzer, quick to recognize his ability, encouraged his harmonies and introduced him to the works of the masters, with special emphasis on Chopin and Debussy. George attended the High School of Commerce for a short period. During that time he was pianist for the morning assembly exercises.

At the age of fifteen and for a consideration of fifteen dollars a week George became a pianist in the "professional department" of Jerome H. Remick and Co., publishers of popular music. He was probably the youngest piano pounder ever employed in Tin Pan Alley. He played all day, travelled to nearby cities to accompany the song pluggers, was sent to vaudeville houses to report which acts were using Remick songs, wrote a tune now and then and, whenever he could, attended concerts. Several of his confreres looked askance at this side of his activities. A song plugger was quite indignant: "I went to a recital once. What's the idea? Why, they only had a piano on the stage."

One day George submitted a song of his own to the professional manager. He was told: "You're here as a pianist, not a writer. We've got plenty of writers under contract." Shortly after, he gave up his job. Soon, at another house, a song of his was accepted. This was in 1916 and the song

17

was called *When You Want 'Em You Can't Get 'Em, When You've Got 'Em You Don't Want 'Em.* George received an advance of five dollars. Murray Roth, who wrote the lyric, was more persuasive and received fifteen. The next published song, written with Sigmund Romberg and Harold Atteridge, was sung in *The Passing Show of 1916.* This also had an arresting title—*Making of a Girl*—and proved pretty conclusively a girlie's looks were greatly dependent on her wearing the proper clothes. As the returns on this song were somewhat less than seven dollars George decided he couldn't live on royalties.

At this stage he became rehearsal pianist for the Dillingham-Ziegfeld production *Miss 1917.* During a Sunday night "concert" at the Century Theatre where *Miss 1917* was playing, Miss Vivienne Segal introduced two of his numbers. These brought him to the attention of Max Dreyfus, then head of Harms, Inc., music publishers. He signed with Dreyfus at thirty-five dollars a week. Although he had many more financially flattering offers he decided his place was with Dreyfus, who was not only a publisher of musical comedies and operettas but also a fine musician and student of the classics. During this time he continued his studies with Edward Kilenyi and then Rubin Goldmark. There was rarely a period in his life when he was not studying. His last teacher was Dr. Joseph Shillinger. I find among the notes of his lessons with Shillinger strange graphs with headings such as "Rhythmic Groups Resulting From the Interference of Several Synchronized Periodicities" and "Groups With the Fractioning Around the Axis of Symmetry."

George began interpolating in various shows. His lyrics were mostly by Irving Caesar. He also began to accept lyrics by Arthur Francis (a pseudonym I concocted from the names of my other brother and my sister) and our first joint effort was a song called *The Real American Folk Song Is a Rag,* which Nora Bayes sang for a while in *Ladies First.* As this piece was more of an essay than a song it didn't get very far. Finally George got a chance to do a show where he was to be sole composer. It was called *Half Past Eight* and advertised a Broadway Beauty Chorus which was nonexistent. With just a few second-hand curtains and sets for production, it opened in Syracuse and was so bad that one critic headed his next morning's review with "Half Past Eight Not Worth Price of War Tax."

A young producer, Alex Aarons, had great faith in George and in 1919 had him do the complete score for *La La Lucille.* This was a smartly conceived musical comedy and the result was quite successful. I recall Victor Jacobi, the light opera composer, telling George, in the Harms elevator, how much he liked its musical subtleties. Jerome Kern also predicted a great future. That same year, 1919, Caesar and George wrote *Swanee,* which, when subsequently introduced by Al Jolson in *Sinbad,* was widely played and purchased.

Beginning in 1920 he wrote, among other things, the music for *George White's Scandals* for five consecutive years. It was for the fourth of this series that he and B. G. DeSylva turned out in six days a short one-act opera called *135th Street.* Lasting only one night it was eliminated not because it was ineffective artistically but because it changed the mood of the audience and the tragic note it injected in the proceedings handicapped the gayer numbers that followed. Intimations of the musical paths George was later to follow, especially in recitative, may be found in *135th Street.* It was also in 1923 that Eva Gauthier, with George at the piano, introduced a group of popular and musical comedy songs at an Aeolian Hall recital. It included numbers by George, Kern, Berlin

19

and Donaldson. Needless to say, this concert caused quite a commotion in musical circles.

Early in 1924, Paul Whiteman announced a concert with new works by Deems Taylor, Victor Herbert and George Gershwin. The newspaper item was the first inkling George had that Whiteman was serious when he had once casually mentioned that some day he expected to do such a concert and hoped for a contribution from George. Finding in his notebooks a theme (the clarinet glissando) which he thought might make an appropriate opening for a more extended work than he had been accustomed to writing, he decided to chance it. Three weeks later, with an orchestration by Ferde Grofé, Whiteman was rehearsing *Rhapsody in Blue* in the night club, Palais Royal. A week later when it was presented at Aeolian Hall with the composer at the piano, the response was immediate. Soon it was being played all over the world.

A year after the *Rhapsody* appeared Walter Damrosch commissioned George to compose a work of symphonic scope for the New York Symphony Society. The *Concerto in F* resulted. Incidentally, this was the first time my brother did his own orchestration; all he had ever done in this line was a number or two in *Primrose,* an operetta he wrote in London. To do the scoring of the *Concerto* George rented a couple of rooms at a hotel in order to have comparative quiet from the noisy and busy private house we lived in with the rest of the family. In those two small hotel rooms, within a period of less than three months, he not only orchestrated this work but worked with me on *Tip-Toes* and at the same time collaborated with Herbert Stothart on *Song of the Flame.* All three works had their premieres within a few days of each other and in addition, Whiteman revived *135th Street* in a concert at Carnegie Hall. With George playing six performances of the *Concerto* during that period under Damrosch in New York, Philadelphia and Baltimore, his energy was seemingly inexhaustible. As he had a very special affection for the *Concerto* it is interesting to note, even if one doesn't believe in artistic yardsticks, that in 1930 when Albert Coates, the eminent English conductor, compiled a list of *Fifty Best Works in Music* there was included only one American work and that was the *Concerto in F.*

For the firm of Aarons and Freedley, beginning in 1924, George and I did the words and music for seven musical comedies, *Lady, Be Good!, Tip-Toes, Oh, Kay!, Funny Face, Treasure Girl, Girl Crazy,* and *Pardon My English;* of these, five were hits and two were failures. In 1926 Edgar Selwyn, having signed George and myself, asked George S. Kaufman if he had an idea for a novel musical. Kaufman said he had a notion for a satire on war, but it probably wouldn't be terribly successful. Selwyn decided to take the chance and *Strike Up the Band* resulted. Out of town it was hailed by the few but the many stayed away. Rewritten by Morrie Ryskind in 1930, it was the first of the three satirical operettas done by the quartet of Kaufman, Ryskind and ourselves. The second, produced by Sam H. Harris, was *Of Thee I Sing,* which was awarded the Pulitzer Prize in 1932 and was followed by *Let 'Em Eat Cake* in 1933.

In the Spring of 1928 George took his fifth and last trip to Europe. With *Funny Face* and *Rosalie* running in New York and *Oh, Kay* in London, a vacation was in order and my sister, my wife and myself accompanied him. I did little other than see sights and drink beer, but George, despite all his social activities, his meetings with many of Europe's important composers, the hours spent with various interviewers and musical critics, still found time to work on *American In Paris* in the hotels we

21

stayed at. The entire "blues" section was written at the Hotel Majestic in Paris. Damrosch sponsored its first performance and it has been popular with symphony organizations ever since.

At the Lewisohn Stadium Concerts in New York George often appeared as soloist, composer and conductor. One program devoted entirely to his own works, August 16, 1932, attracted an audience of over 18,000 and set a record for this stadium. At this concert he introduced *Rhumba* (later called *Cuban Overture*) which Pitts Sanborn found superior to Ravel's *Bolero* in musical body. At Ravinia Park and other stadia and concert halls his appearance usually broke local records for attendance. In 1934 he toured with an orchestra conducted by Charles Previn and gave thirty concerts in as many days. In the year 1936 he had more performances of his works played by symphonic organizations than did any other American composer. The greatest gathering ever to crowd the Lewisohn Stadium attended the Memorial Concert in August, 1937.

Porgy and Bess, his most ambitious work, was composed in eleven months and he did the orchestration in nine; during this period he also did a good deal of broadcasting. Although most of the opera was done in New York, parts were written in Charleston's Folly Beach, in Westchester, in Palm Beach, in Fire Island and in the Adirondacks. Sponsored by The Theatre Guild, directed by Rouben Mamoulian and conducted by Alexander Smallens, it opened in Boston to great acclaim, then played sixteen weeks in New York and followed with a three months' road tour. In 1938 Merle Armitage revived it in Los Angeles and San Francisco with most of the original cast.

Besides his music, George was also interested in painting. He became an ardent collector, specializing in the French moderns and in African sculpture. About 1928 he himself began to paint, and was considered exceedingly capable by professional critics.

Hollywood called again in the Summer of 1936 (we had been there in 1930 for the picture *Delicious*) and the Astaire-Rogers film *Shall We Dance?* resulted. This was followed by *A Damsel in Distress* and we were working on *The Goldwyn Follies* when George began to get the headaches which three weeks later proved to be caused by a tumor in the brain. He never learned during that period that he had just been elected an honorary member of the Academy of Santa Cecilia, Rome—Italy's highest award to foreign composers. We didn't bother him with correspondence although two days before the operation we were still discussing songs. He died Sunday morning, July 11, 1937, in Los Angeles at the age of 38.

1938 · PAUL WHITEMAN

There is an especial place in my heart reserved for George Gershwin, and that place is his alone. Before Gershwin there were hundreds of great song writers. They were not inartistic in their compositions, but they had not touched the field that awaited his particular genius. What I am attempting to say is that there was nothing in their contributions from the technical side of music or musical development that would give reason for the so-called jazz type to be included in the concert field. It remained for Gershwin to give dignity to a medium of expression that had before him been held in slight contempt. His rare originality, coupled with his keen grasp of the orchestra, always was shown in his piano playing. He thought always in orchestral terms, and he played in that fashion.

He was the perfect wedding of man who could write a hit—something that caught and held the public fancy—and still make it a composition worthy of the concert field's earnest attention. His *Rhapsody in Blue* is a graphic example. No one can hear it without feeling its power, even those who profess to have an appreciation for better music. The *Rhapsody* is a hit, and yet technically excellent.

I feel that George Gershwin was more than ever just commencing to come into his own. With his knowledge and skill he wrote numbers that have become musical milestones. He was a great example of the merging of hit qualities with intelligent musicianship.

He led the way. He has given the finer jazz a firm root—so firm a root that others who come after him may carry on his fine tradition. The Gershwin *theme* has been inculcated in the minds of the younger composers, and it is for them to take it, and go forward.

I shall go back a number of years to trace the history of how George Gershwin came to write *Rhapsody in Blue* for me. Brought up as I was in the symphonic field, I could never understand why jazz had to be a haphazard thing. I recall that in San Francisco I heard bands render one number in excellent style and another in the worst possible manner. They were faking, or as we say today, jamming. It occurred to me that the scores of those could be written, and if I have contributed anything to music, it is that one thing. I started the arranging business among the bands.

But to get along. All the years that I was playing jazz, I never stopped wanting to go into concert halls and in some measure remove the stigma of barbaric strains and jungle cacophony from jazz. During that time I was associated with Gershwin and Victor Herbert. George was working in a publishing house, although he had had *Swanee* and several other hits to his credit.

We talked about my idea. "All you have to do is hire a hall," Herbert told me. He was sympathetic. He always was with anything revolutionary.

I felt that George could write the thing I needed. Something that would show that jazz had progressed. Something that would illustrate that it was a great deal more than savage rhythm from the jungle. Something that would give expression to what I was seeking to bring out.

"I'll write it as a rhapsody," George said. "We don't want to be bound down. We'll lay ourselves open to criticism if we do. I'll write a *Rhapsody in Blue*."

25

Well, we mulled over it. And, as young fellows will, I guess we talked too much about it. Another leader got word of it, and reports came to me that he was going to do the thing we had been talking about. I certainly didn't want to see a brainchild of mine ruined, so I called up Aeolian Hall and made arrangements for a concert within twenty-four days.

George came running to me. "What's this I hear, Paul? You're going to do this thing in twenty-four days? I'd planned to take six months with it. But if it's twenty-four days, it's twenty-four days, and I'll do it."

He probably had given it some thought, but only the fact that he was a genius and a tireless worker enabled him to turn out the *Rhapsody* in that short space of time.

We orchestrated it a sheet at a time as it came in. George would complete a page, and we'd orchestrate it. That went on until it was completed. And mind you, it was so perfect that it never has been changed.

The time came for the concert. How well I remember! A friend gave a luncheon for us. Neither of us could eat. But that night in Aeolian Hall I knew we were set. The audience was electric. You can feel those things in the back of your neck. I felt it then. Critics were there—the best. But they weren't antagonistic. They were friendly. It was in the air.

Somewhere about the middle of the score I began crying. When I came to myself, I was eleven pages along, and until this day I cannot tell you how I conducted that far. Afterward, George, who was playing with us, told me he experienced the same sensation. He cried, too.

The rest is history.

George Gershwin was the highest type of character. He is gone—but his music is his enduring monument.

FERDE
1938·GROFÉ

It was in 1920 that I first met George Gershwin, who came to a rehearsal
at the Palais Royal in New York, a night club where I was then a member
of the Paul Whiteman orchestra as its pianist and arranger. George had
already written music for one or two productions of *George White's
Scandals,* and came to hear its song-hit (called *Drifting With The Tide,*
I believe) in the version I had adapted for the Whiteman organization.
The young composer was extremely modest and grateful, and expressed
his pleasure and thanks for what I had done with his piece.

That was the beginning of a close friendship with George which
lasted until his untimely death. The Palais Royal episode was followed
by many meetings at the publishing establishment of Harms, which sponsored my arrangements of all the outstanding Gershwin numbers, played
by Whiteman and recorded by Victor. Meanwhile, too, I encountered
George often at Buddy DeSylva's apartment, and there I first heard the
former's one-act Negro opera, *135th Street* or *Blue Monday.* It was
played by the creator, and hummed by DeSylva. Even with such a crude
performance, the work struck me as highly original and as representing
a new departure in American music. Later I re-scored the opera for production with Whiteman at his 1936 Carnegie Hall concert, in New
York, where the only stage-props were tables and chairs, and Benny Fields
and Blossom Seeley did the leading rôles.

27

Finally George was inspired to compose his *Rhapsody in Blue,* and just after that our real intimacy developed. He lived with his parents and brothers and sister, all of them children, except Ira, and I practically lived too at their uptown Amsterdam Avenue and 110th Street apartment, for I called there daily for more pages of George's masterpiece, which he originally composed in two-piano form. He and his brother Ira had a back room where there was an upright piano, and that is where the *Rhapsody* grew into being.

During that time I learned to value the atmosphere of George's home, and the sweet hospitality of his mother and father. Mrs. Gershwin watched our labors with loving interest, and taught me to appreciate Russian tea, which she brewed for us when we rested.

I like to think that I had something to do with the Whiteman desire to premiere the *Rhapsody,* for I raved to him about it enthusiastically until the day he accepted it for performance. Some years later, a story was published about a feud supposed to exist between George and me regarding the *Rhapsody,* saying that he claimed I had done little in the scoring of the work, after he had provided me with his own practically complete orchestration. The story was, of course, entirely untrue, and George immediately denied it publicly. At that time he could not orchestrate, but being ambitious, he was already studying the art with Rubin Goldmark, and subsequently acquired facility. I orchestrated the *Rhapsody* from the composer's sketch for two pianos, and still have his autographed manuscript in my possession. In early 1933 I called at his Riverside Drive penthouse for the partiture of his *2nd Rhapsody,* which I re-scored for Whiteman's 1933 New York concert, and that was one of my last visits with George. My final glimpse of him came at the New York dinner to Harry

Hirshfield about two years ago, when I conducted excerpts from *Porgy and Bess.* On that occasion he was kind enough to say that I made a wise move when I left Whiteman to go into the baton profession on my own, and he also made me blush with his warm praise of my composition, *Metropolis,* in which he singled out the "fugato" measures for special compliment.

The news of George's death came as a dreadful shock to me, and I received it with a sense of irreparable loss, for I was deprived of a dear friend, and America of a unique and grandly gifted composer. It is not over-estimating his music to say that it expressed something distinctly new, something typically of our land and people, and employed an unmistakable American idiom in melody, rhythm, and harmonization. George Gershwin left an indelible impression on our native music, and the proof is, that he has had many imitators, but none who could successfully duplicate his genius.

I own candidly that Gershwin influenced me too in my compositions, both through his own examples, and because he encouraged me so warmly. If I had not come so close to his personality and musical thought, I doubt whether I would have gone on and written in the larger forms.

I set down these lines, therefore, as a tribute of love and thankfulness, and in the full realization that I may never again meet the like of George Gershwin, a rare and refined spirit, an innovator in American music, and one who has left upon it a lasting imprint of new ideas voiced with bold originality.

W I L L I A M
1933·D A L Y

In The American Spectator for December appears an article by Allan Lincoln Langley, entitled "The Gershwin Myth," in which the author definitely tries to convey to the reader the idea that Gershwin is not the orchestrator, and probably not the author, of the works attributed to him. I am signally honored by being mentioned as a probable "ghost writer," as attest the following:

"As for *An American in Paris,* the genial Daly was constantly in rehearsal attendance, both as répétiteur and adviser, and any member of the orchestra could testify that he knew far more about the score than Gershwin. The point is that no previous claimant to honors in symphonic composition has ever presented so much argument and so much controversy as to whether his work was his own or not."

I thank Mr. Langley for the compliment, but I neither wrote nor orchestrated the *American.* My only contribution consisted of a few suggestions about reinforcing the scoring here and there, and I'm not sure that Gershwin, probably with good reason, accepted them. But, then, Gershwin receives many such suggestions from his many friends to whom he always plays his various compositions, light or symphonic, while they are in the process of being written. Possibly Mr. Langley feels that we all get together (and we'd have to meet in the Yankee Stadium) and write Mr. Gershwin's music for him.

I would be only too happy to be known as the composer of *An American in Paris,* or of any of Gershwin's works, or as the orchestrator of them. But, alas! I am by trade a conductor (and because Gershwin thinks I am a good one, especially for his music, maybe Mr. Langley has been thrown off the scent). It is true that I orchestrate many Gershwin numbers for the theatre; but so does Russell Bennett. And I have reduced some of his symphonic works for smaller orchestra for use on the radio. And it is true that we are close friends — to my great profit — and that I use that relationship to criticize. But this is far from the rôle that Mr. Langley suggests.

In fine, the fact is that I have never written one note of any of his compositions, or so much as orchestrated one whole bar of any one of his symphonic works.

Mr. Langley's asseverations are of importance only through the fact that they are now published and are sent abroad in the world to influence those who have no means of checking up on the facts, and to give comfort to those who want to think that Gershwin is a myth.

I suppose I should really resent the fact that Langley attributes Gershwin's work to me, since Langley finds all of it so bad. But fortunately for my amour propre, I have heard some of Langley's compositions. He really should stay away from ink and stick to his viola.

1938 · WALTER DAMROSCH

It was in 1925 that I first became attracted by George Gershwin and the music which he had composed for various Broadway productions. It showed such originality both of melodic invention and harmonic progressions that I strongly felt that he had in him the possibility of development on more serious lines.

I suggested to the president of the New York Symphony Society, Mr. Harry Harkness Flagler, that it might be a lovely and important inducement for his artistic future to commission him to write a piano concerto for the Symphony Society, which should have its first performance at one of our concerts, he to play the piano part. Mr. Flagler heartily agreed with this suggestion and George Gershwin wrote the concerto for us and received almost unanimous and enthusiastic acclaim for the work on its production on December 3, 1925. I still think that the second movement of this concerto, with its dreamy atmosphere of a summer night in a garden of our South, reaches a high water mark of his talent.

I developed a strong affection for him personally, and for the genuineness of his musical talent. He had an almost child-like affection and pride for his own music. To tell the truth, I tried to wean him, so to speak, from Broadway, as I felt that he had it in him to develop on more serious lines than the Broadway musical shows demanded or even permitted. But the lure of the lighter forms in which he had become such a master, proved too strong. Perhaps I was wrong and his own instinct guided him towards what he felt most able to do. In the end it must be an inner urge which compels our artistic destinies.

1935·DUBOSE HEYWARD

Nothing could be more ill-advised than the writing of this article. It exhibits all too clearly the decay of a human will, and it is strewn with the debris of broken resolutions. Out of a limited but illuminating Broadway experience, I have grasped the simple fact that a play does not exist until the critics and the public have looked upon it and found it good. Could there then be a more perfect example of artless, parental exhibitionism than the spectacle of a playwright prattling about his expected brain-child a full month before the hazardous accouchement?

How did it happen? I will tell you. I can at least expose the system of which I am a victim.

You leave the first rehearsal, hypnotized by the music of your own words. You are beguiled into the sanctum of an editor. Your fingers close of their own volition about a cocktail glass. You are told things about your work which, in your state of initial intoxication, you are fatuous enough to believe. You conclude that the editor is also a discriminating critic and altogether an excellent fellow. And then, since, in any event it is against nature for an author to say "no" to an editor, you find yourself committed. It is not until later that you realize your deadline for a monthly periodical is a month in advance of publication, and that your story may burst from the presses, not as a bright paean for the living, but a sad and ironical epitaph for the dead.

34

But the story of *Porgy* has a definite past, as well as a projected reincarnation, and the production of the opera is the materialization of an idea suggested by George Gershwin in a letter written to me nine years ago. The drama had not yet been produced, but was being written by my wife, Dorothy Heyward, and myself for the Theatre Guild, when George read the novel and suggested a meeting.

My first impression of my collaborator remains with me and is singularly vivid. A young man of enormous physical and emotional vitality, who possessed the faculty of seeing himself quite impersonally and realistically, and who knew exactly what he wanted and where he was going. This characteristic put him beyond both modesty and conceit. About himself he would merely mention certain facts, aspirations, failings. They were usually right.

We discussed *Porgy*. He said that it would not matter about the dramatic production, as it would be a number of years before he would be prepared technically to compose an opera. At the time he had numerous Broadway successes to his credit, and his *Rhapsody in Blue,* published three years before, had placed him in the front rank of American composers. It was extraordinary, I thought, that, in view of a success that might well have dazzled any man, he could appraise his talent with such complete detachment. And so we decided then that some day when we were both prepared we would do an operatic version of my simple Negro beggar of the Charleston streets.

In the meantime, the play went into rehearsal at the Guild Theatre. Rouben Mamoulian, in his first appearance on Broadway, was entrusted with its direction. A cast was assembled from Negro night clubs and Harlem theatres. Then for six weeks, what we all believed to be Broadway's

35

most highly speculative venture dragged its personnel through the extremes of hope and despair toward the opening night.

I suppose it is sheer physical exhaustion, plus the emotional bludgeoning an author undergoes during rehearsals, that reduces him to pessimistic witlessness on the night of the premiere. Out of that night, I remember only vaguely a few moments of startling beauty: Mamoulian's fantastic shadows, the heartbreaking quality of the funeral spiritual, Porgy's pathetic leave taking. But never to be forgotten was that awful moment when Crown shouted to the silent heavens, "Gawd laugh and Crown laugh back." Then, after an aching interval, came the belated clap of thunder that was supposed to be the laugh of God. The scene shifts seemed interminable. And lastly, and most crushing as we cowered at the back of the house under the protective wing of Philip Moeller, came the exit of Woollcott before the last scene of the play.

I have never seen him since, but I could point him out immediately in any crowd, so vivid is my impression of him. He stands about forty feet in his stockings, is about thirty feet broad; and when he rises to his full height from the second row in the orchestra, he can blot out an entire proscenium arch. His mouth is that of a medieval executioner, and when he strides down a theatre aisle and past a terror-stricken playwright, his footsteps shake the building with the tread of doom. Somebody might have warned us that he had an early deadline, and had to get his copy in, but nobody did. To us it was a walk-out. He gave us a fine review. He proved that dramatic critics really are omniscient by knowing how the show ended. But the mischief had been done. Thirty months later, when the play closed after a run in America and a successful journey across the Atlantic, the authors were still more or less nervous wrecks.

Time passed and Porgy and the goat lay comfortably dossed down in Cain's warehouse. But every year, between novels with me, and Broadway productions with George, I would journey North and we would meet and discuss our opera. I remember George saying once—it was, I think, when he was planning to stage *An American in Paris*—that he would stay abroad and put in some intensive study in counterpoint. As always, he knew just where he was going. The success of his symphonic poem in Paris was flattering, but the main idea was to build toward the opera.

Later he worked with Joseph Schillinger, the musicologist, who carried him from Bach to Schoenberg, concentrating his attention on polytonality—modern harmony, and counterpoint.

And then in October, exactly two years ago, our impatience got the better of what may prove to have been our better judgment, and the actual adventure of composing began.

It is the fashion in America to lament the prostitution of art by the big magazine, the radio, the moving pictures. With this I have little patience. Properly utilized, the radio and the pictures may be to the present-day writer what his prince was to Villon, the king of Bavaria was to Wagner.

At no other time has it been possible for a writer to earn by hiring himself out as a skilled technician for, say, two months, sufficient income to sustain him for a year. And yet the moving pictures have made it possible. I decided that the silver screen should be my Maecenas, and George elected to serve the radio.

During my first year I wrote the screen version of *The Emperor Jones*. For this I may have lost the friendship of Eugene O'Neill. I haven't dared

37

to look him up since. And to finance my second year I made a pilgrimage to Hollywood to tinker at Pearl Buck's *Good Earth.* My selection for this assignment presented a perfect example of motion picture logic. When I arrived on the lot and asked why I had been offered the job, it was made perfectly plain to me. Negroes were not a Caucasian people. Neither were Chinamen. I wrote understandingly of Negroes. It was obvious then that I would understand the Chinese. I suspect that before my engagement closed their faith in their reasoning power was shaken. But I gave them my best, and when I left for the East I was free to complete my work on the opera.

Statistics record the fact that there are 25,000,000 radios in America. Their contribution to the opera was indirect but important. Out of them for half an hour each week poured the glad tidings that Feenamint could be wheedled away from virtually any drug clerk in America for one dime —the tenth part of a dollar. And with the authentic medicine-man flair, the manufacturer distributed his information in an irresistible wrapper of Gershwin hits, with the composer at the piano.

There is, I imagine, a worse fate than that which derives from the use of a laxative gum. And, anyhow, we felt that the end justified the means, and that they also served who only sat and waited.

At the outset we were faced by a difficult problem. I was firm in my refusal to leave the South and live in New York. Gershwin was bound for the duration of his contract to the microphone at Radio City. The matter of effecting a happy union between words and music across a thousand miles of Atlantic seaboard baffled us for a moment. The solution came quite naturally when we associated Ira Gershwin with us. Presently we evolved a system by which, between my visits North, or George's

38

dash to Charleston, I could send scenes and lyrics. Then the brothers Gershwin, after their extraordinary fashion, would get at the piano, pound, wrangle, swear, burst into weird snatches of song, and eventually emerge with a polished lyric. Then too, Ira's gift for the more sophisticated lyric was exactly suited to the task of writing the songs for Sporting Life, the Harlem gambler who had drifted into Catfish Row.

I imagine that in after years when George looks back upon this time, he will feel that the summer of 1934 furnished him with one of the most satisfying as well as exciting experiences of his career. Under the baking suns of July and August we established ourselves on Folly Island, a small barrier island ten miles from Charleston. James Island with its large population of primitive Gullah Negroes lay adjacent, and furnished us with a laboratory in which to test our theories, as well as an inexhaustible source of folk material. But the most interesting discovery to me, as we sat listening to their spirituals, or watched a group shuffling before a cabin or country store, was that to George it was more like a homecoming than an exploration. The quality in him which had produced the *Rhapsody in Blue* in the most sophisticated city in America, found its counterpart in the impulse behind the music and bodily rhythms of the simple Negro peasant of the South.

The Gullah Negro prides himself on what he calls "shouting." This is a complicated rhythmic pattern beaten out by feet and hands as an accompaniment to the spirituals, and is indubitably an African survival. I shall never forget the night when, at a Negro meeting on a remote sea-island, George started "shouting" with them. And eventually to their huge delight stole the show from their champion "shouter." I think that he is probably the only white man in America who could have done it.

Another night as we were about to enter a dilapidated cabin that had been taken as a meeting house by a group of Negro Holy Rollers, George caught my arm and held me. The sound that had arrested him was one to which, through long familiarity, I attached no special importance. But now, listening to it with him, and noticing his excitement, I began to catch its extraordinary quality. It consisted of perhaps a dozen voices raised in loud rhythmic prayer. The odd thing about it was that while each had started at a different time, upon a different theme, they formed a clearly defined rhythmic pattern, and that this, with the actual words lost, and the inevitable pounding of the rhythm, produced an effect almost terrifying in its primitive intensity. Inspired by the extraordinary effect, George wrote six simultaneous prayers producing a terrifying primitive invocation to God in the face of the hurricane.

We had hoped, and it was logical, that the Theatre Guild would produce the opera. An excursion into that field of the theatre was a new idea to the directors. But then they had gambled once on *Porgy* and won. There was a sort of indulgent affection for the cripple and his goat on Fifty-second Street. Most certainly they did not want anybody else to do it, and so contracts were signed.

Having committed themselves, the Guild proceeded to deprive us of all alibis in the event of failure by giving us a free hand in the casting and a star producing staff.

Mamoulian returned from Hollywood to assume the direction. (Alexander Smallens, who had conducted the Philharmonic Stadium Concerts, and the Philadelphia Symphony, and who, in spite of having conducted the orchestra of *Four Saints in Three Acts,* still made his wants known in comprehensible English, was made conductor.)

40

Alexander Steinert, pianist and composer, with a Prix de Rome to his credit, was intrusted with the coaching of the principals.

For a year George had been cast-hunting. It had been an exciting, if at times a strenuous sport. But last April, when I journeyed North to hear the aspirants and advise on the final decisions, I was amazed at the amount of promising talent exhibited. The cast was assembled. Steinert took them in hand, and at the first rehearsal he had them ready to read the difficult score from beginning to end.

We were in rather a dither about the name. The composer and author both felt that the opera should be called simply *Porgy*. But there was a feeling in the publicity department that this would lead to a confusion in that amorphous region known as the public mind, and that *Porgy* in lights might be construed as a revival of the original play, rather than as the Gershwin opus.

There had of course been *Pelleas and Melisande, Samson and Delilah, Tristan and Isolde.*

"And so," said Heyward, with the humility characteristic of those who draw their sustenance from the theatre, "why not *Porgy and Bess?*"

To which Gershwin replied with the detachment to which I have referred and which could not possibly be mistaken for conceit, "Of course, it's right in the operatic tradition."

Two years! It doesn't seem that long. There has been so much to do. The published version of the piano and vocal score, fresh from the press, runs to five hundred and sixty pages. And when that was finished, George tackled the orchestration single handed. The resulting manuscript is impressive. It contains seven hundred pages of closely written music, and it is the fruit of nine months of unremitting labor.

41

For my own part, I had a play which needed to be cut forty per cent for the libretto, yet nothing of dramatic value could be sacrificed. The dialogue had to follow that of the drama, but it had to be arranged to form a new pattern, to escape monotony and adapt itself to the music. And then there were the spirituals, and the lyrics upon which Ira and I worked.

In the theatre every production is a gamble. In some, naturally, the odds are greater than in others. *Porgy and Bess* has, I believe, a fair chance of scoring. But whether it does or not, we who have written and composed the opera cannot lose. We have spent two years doing exactly what we wanted to. It has been a very especial sort of adventure. That, at any rate, is in the bag.

ALEXANDER
1938·STEINERT

It was merely by chance that I happened to be at a reception in honor of Strawinsky, given by the League of Composers at the Town Hall in New York during the winter of 1935. A slight tap of the shoulder caused me to turn around. It was George Gershwin.

"Haven't you been coaching the singers of the Russian Opera Company recently?" he asked. "Seeing you here reminds me that I have no one to coach my new opera, *Porgy*. Would it interest you to do it?" It did not take me long to decide. The next day I signed an agreement with the Theatre Guild, and thus began my association with *Porgy and Bess,* and at the same time one of the most inspiring friendships of my life.

It is rare to combine work and play with the same person, but in this instance it was hard to say where the one ended and the other began. From then on I saw George Gershwin nearly every day. We sat for many hours, listening to hundreds of auditions, for it was no easy task to choose the right cast for the opera. The types had to be marked, the voices satisfactory. Many of the colored people, born and educated in the North, hadn't the slightest trace of the essential Negro lingo, and were obliged to learn the dialect of the South. Some had had a superior training in the finest music schools of the country; others were unable to read a note and had to learn their rôles by ear. Mr. Gershwin, having made an exhaustive study of the Negroes in Charleston, often astonished the company by showing them

43

how to interpret their parts authentically. I little realized then that subsequently I should be called upon to succeed Alexander Smallens, the original conductor of the opera, when he left to fulfill engagements with the Philadelphia Orchestra, and that ultimately I should conduct over a hundred performances of *Porgy and Bess* in nine cities throughout the country.

During the summer months of rehearsing, Gershwin completed the orchestration of the score, every page of which he did himself. He deserves particular credit for the way in which he applied himself to the study of music. It sufficed that someone else orchestrated his *Rhapsody in Blue.* By the time he had composed his next work, he had acquired sufficient knowledge to do all his own orchestrating thereafter.

There was a great bond which united all those connected with the opera — a kind of fraternity which seemed to exist between the members of the company, the authors, the stage directors, and the producers. It was as noticeable at the recent revival on the Pacific Coast as in the first production. Largely responsible for this was the guiding hand of Rouben Mamoulian, who staged the original play for the Theatre Guild in 1927. His intuitive understanding, his imagination, and the great sympathy for those he was working with obtained immediate response from the actors and singers.

It would be difficult to imagine *Porgy and Bess* without Todd Duncan and Anne Brown in the title roles, Ruby Elzy as Serena, Georgette Harvey as Maria, and Bubbles, or his successor, Avon Long, as Sportin' Life. As to Eva Jessye's choir, it may well serve as an example of what can be accomplished on the operatic stage.

At this point a few words might be said about the difficulties *Porgy and Bess* has had to encounter. An opera in every sense of the word, even

44

in spite of its lighter moments, it has suffered from being treated as a theatrical production. It belongs in an opera house, played by a large orchestra, for which it was written. Had it been done in this way, however, it would only have had three or four performances, and it was destined to run extensively in the East and West and on the road. For this reason it was performed in legitimate theatres with orchestra pits of small seating capacity.

As an opera, it is constantly being compared to the original theatrical production as presented by the Theatre Guild of New York in 1927. From the start one should disassociate the two. The limitations and drawbacks of opera are only too well known to be dwelt upon here, and it is only thanks to George Gershwin's expert treatment that so much of the original flavor has remained. It is a work which appeals to the masses, who feel in it something which is typically American — the vibrant gayety of Broadway and Harlem, the nostalgia of the South, as depicted by a composer whose racial background and environment enabled him to understand these things so well. It was not without reason that he referred to *Porgy* as a folk-opera, and wished it to be known as such.

One of George Gershwin's greatest qualities was his complete belief in what he was doing, and this was not always appreciated and understood by those who did not know him well. He knew he had something to say, and he said it. He was always open to conviction, however, and frankly admitted when he felt he had fallen short of the goal he had set. He was distinctly ambitious, and no one can say what his next major work might have been. When one examines the first operatic attempts of Wagner, Verdi, or Puccini, one can justly be enthusiastic about Gershwin's first opera.

He will always exert a great influence upon those who were fortunate enough to know him intimately. He was a great perfectionist, and whatever he undertook he did well, whether it was painting, photography, or sports. In the latter years of his life, his love for modern painting was a dominant factor, and the logical outcome of his aesthetic development.

His courage about his own work was great. When *Porgy and Bess* was first produced, it lasted well over three hours. Very few composers, if any, would have stood by and witnessed with comparative calm the dismemberment of their brain-child until it had been reduced by nearly a quarter! He was quite philosophical about it, realizing that it was better for the continuity and success of the work.

George's relationship with his brother Ira was a most interesting one, and more than by blood. Each had a profound influence on the other; each completed the other. When they collaborated on popular music, George's understanding of the lyrics equalled his brother's feeling for music. They worked with an amazing rapidity and seemingly without effort, although those close to them knew how often they would struggle over a single phrase. It is interesting to review George Gershwin's Song Book and note how many of the early numbers are still performed. In many cases one has forgotten that it was he who wrote them — they have just become old friends who are taken for granted. Isn't this music, with its dance rhythms, the nearest approach we have to American Folk Music—this music which so completely typifies our country? And may it not be rightly compared to the corresponding Russian, Irish, or Hungarian folk tunes? Many years will pass before *Summertime* and *The Man I Love* are forgotten, and they will live long after other American music has ceased to be.

1938·ROUBEN MAMOULIAN

The first time I met George Gershwin was in late 1923 in Rochester, N. Y., where I had recently arrived from Europe to direct operas at the Eastman Theatre. One evening I was asked to join some friends at a little place called the Corner Club. Among them I found Gene Goossens, the English conductor, Artur Rubinstein, the pianist, and a slim young man whom I had never met before. He was introduced as George Gershwin, the songwriter. After an interlude of conversation, sandwiches and beer, Artur Rubinstein played the piano. He played brilliantly some of the great classic composers. When he finished we asked Gershwin to play for us. He willingly agreed and played several of his popular melodies with that sparkling vitality and fascinating rhythmic punctuations, the secret of which he knew so well. Among the songs he played was that humorous ditty *Misha, Yasha, Tasha, Sasha,* which always remained one of his favorites in spite of the fact that it had never been generally published. (Curious that the first time I met George he played this ditty and he played it again the last time I saw him, which was a few days before his death.) After having played his popular songs to our great enjoyment, Gershwin said that he had been working on something that he hoped would reach the concert stage. He was a little shy about playing it in front of Artur Rubinstein. However, we insisted, so he played parts of that new composition. I will never forget the novelty and freshness of that

47

music—its marvelous colors and rhythmic variations and the strength and authority that underlined it. After he had finished playing, I asked him, "What are you going to call this, Mr. Gershwin?" He said, "I thought I'd call it *Rhapsody in Blue*" ...

A few months later he played it to a sensational reception in Carnegie Hall.

My first impression of Gershwin during that evening was that of a rather worried and anxious young man—very ambitious and not very happy. Rather reserved and self-centered and in some curious way suspicious of the world, looking not unlike a child with more apples than he can comfortably hold in his hands and afraid that someone would take them away from him.

I did not see Gershwin again until years later when I started working on *Porgy and Bess.* I was in Hollywood directing motion pictures when I heard that George was going to use *Porgy* as a libretto for his first opera. At first I was shocked. I felt the play was so pure and complete in its form, had such a direct simplicity and strength, that any attempt to translate it into operatic form might spoil it. However, my second thought was that if there was a composer in the whole world equipped by the quality of his talent to achieve this task, George was that composer.

When the score was completed I was still on the coast. The Theatre Guild and George asked me to come back to New York and direct the opera. The score couldn't be sent to me in Hollywood because George was busy orchestrating it, but I felt so sure that it would be exciting and beautiful, that I signed a contract with the Guild without having heard a single note of what I was to direct.

George was particularly keen to orchestrate the score all by himself.

He worked very long and hard at it. He wrote me in a letter, "I am orchestrating the opera at the present time and have about five months' work left. It is really a tremendous task scoring three hours of music." It was, and he did it. (And his was such a beautiful-looking manuscript!)

I finally arrived in New York and on the first evening I was to hear George's score. I met George and Ira in the Gershwin apartment. All three of us were very excited. George and Ira were obviously anxious for me to like the music. As for me, I was even more anxious. You see, I loved the story of *Porgy* and every single character in it; I loved its changing moods, its sadness and its gaiety, its passion and its tenderness, and all the emotional richness of the Negro soul expressed in it. *Porgy,* the play, having been my very first production in New York, meant a great deal to me. I felt about it the way I imagine a mother feels about her first-born. If it were to be "clothed" in music I was jealously anxious for that music to be good. It had to be good!

It was rather amusing how all three of us were trying to be nonchalant and poised that evening, yet we were trembling with excitement. The brothers handed me a tall highball and put me in a comfortable leather armchair. George sat down at the piano while Ira stood over him like a guardian angel. George's hands went up in the air about to strike the shining keys. Half-way down, he changed his mind, turned to me and said, "Of course, Rouben, you must understand it's very difficult to play this score. As a matter of fact, it's really impossible! Can you play Wagner on the piano? Well, this is just like Wagner!" I assured George that I understood. Up went his nervous hands again and the next second I was listening to the opening "piano music" of the opera. I found it so exciting, so full of color and so provocative in its rhythm that after this first piano

49

section was over, I jumped out of my armchair and interrupted George to tell him how much I liked it. Both brothers were as happy as children to hear words of praise, though heaven knows, they should have been used to them by then. When my explosion was over and they went back to the piano, they both blissfully closed their eyes before they continued with the lovely *Summertime* song. George played with the most beatific smile on his face. He seemed to float on the waves of his own music with the southern sun shining on him. Ira sang—he threw his head back with abandon, his eyes closed, and sang like a nightingale! In the middle of the song George couldn't bear it any longer and took over the singing from him. To describe George's face while he sang *Summertime* is something that is beyond my capacity as a writer. "Nirvana" might be the word! So it went on. George was the orchestra and sang half of the parts, Ira sang the other half. Ira was also frequently the "audience." It was touching to see how he, while singing, would become so overwhelmed with admiration for his brother, that he would look from him to me with half-open eyes and pantomime with a soft gesture of his hand, as if saying, "*He* did it. Isn't it wonderful? Isn't *he* wonderful?" George would frequently take his eyes away from the score and watch me covertly and my reaction to the music while pretending that he wasn't really doing it at all. It was very late into the night before we finished with the opera and sometimes I think that in a way that was the best performance of it I ever heard. We all felt exultantly happy. The next morning both George and Ira had completely lost their voices. For two days they couldn't talk, they only whispered. I shall never forget that evening—the enthusiasm of the two brothers about the music, their anxiety to do it justice, their joy at its being appreciated and with it all their touching devotion for each other. It is one of those rare tender memories one so cherishes in life.

50

The first day of rehearsing a play is always difficult. It is like break-ing mountains of ice. The end of it leaves one completely exhausted and usually a little depressed. Everything seems awkward, disorganized, al-most hopeless. That's the way I felt after the first day of *Porgy and Bess*. I lay in my bed in my apartment at the Navarro and was indulging in rather melancholy and misanthropic thoughts. Suddenly the phone rang and George Gershwin was announced. This delighted me as I felt in need of encouragement and kind words. I picked up the receiver and said "Hello" with eager anticipation. George's voice came glowing with enthusiasm: "Rouben, I couldn't help calling you . . . I just *had* to call you and tell you how I feel. I am so thrilled and delighted over the rehearsal today." (My heart started warming up and I already began to feel better!) "Of course," he went on, "I always knew that *Porgy and Bess* was wonderful, but I never thought I'd feel the way I feel now. I tell you, after listening to that rehearsal today, I think the music is so marvelous—I really don't believe I wrote it!"

George's attitude towards himself and his work was apt to be misun-derstood by people who did not know him well. Because he liked his own music and praised himself, some of them thought he was conceited. This was not so, as I myself discovered. Conceit is made of much sterner stuff —it was not that with George. It was his faculty to look at himself and his work in just as detached a manner as if he were looking at somebody else. George had a tremendous capacity for appreciation and enthusiasm and always gave it generous expression in words. Whatever he liked, he praised. He happened to like his own music too, so he praised it without any self-consciousness or false modesty. It seems to me that this sense of exaggerated modesty in artists is highly overrated by people. It is made out to be a saintly virtue where frequently it is merely sanctimonious and actually nothing but masked vanity and conceit. Very often people who seem so modest about their work would all but tear you to pieces if you suggested cutting anything out of what they had written, considering every word of it as well-nigh sacred. Yet George, who loved his own stuff as much as he did, never hesitated to make any cuts that were necessary. *Porgy and Bess* as performed in New York was almost forty-five minutes shorter than the original score. He did this because he had no false vanity about his work and also because George was one of the best showmen I have ever known. He knew the theatre, he knew the audience. His showmanship was so keen that no matter how well he loved a musical passage or an aria (like the Buzzard song in *Porgy and Bess,* for instance), he would cut it out without hesitation if that improved the performance as a whole. This makes me think of the most charming and intangible present I have ever received on my birthday. It was on October 8, 1935 —after a rehearsal during which we cut the piano passage out of the opera. George presented me with a sheet of paper on which he wrote the opening bars of that passage and inscribed, "Here Rouben is a little birthday present for you—the 'cut' piano music. George Gershwin."

George was so completely naïve and innocent in his liking of his own work that it actually became one of the endearing qualities of his nature. Some little expressions that would seem arrogant coming from other men were touching and lovable when coming from George. I remember once I had to meet George and several other friends for dinner in a restaurant across the street from the Guild Theatre. I was late, so I went there unshaven and rather haggard-looking. I apologized to the company for my appearance. George said, "Rouben, don't apologize. Personally, I love you when you're unshaven." "Why, George?" I asked. "Because," said he, "when you're unshaven you look like me."

Another time we were having lunch at Lindy's after a morning's rehearsal which George had attended. As we sat there I started, for some unknown reason, humming an air out of Rimsky-Korsakow. George stopped eating, turned to me with a very shocked expression on his face and said, "Rouben, I think this is terrible! You have just been rehearsing my music and here you are humming some Russian melodies. Why do you do that?" At first, I thought George was joking, but then I saw the hurt look in his eyes and knew he was in dead earnest. So I said, "George, I am very sorry. I don't know why I did it." The lunch went on, but George didn't touch his food for quite a while, looking very depressed. Then suddenly his face lighted up with a smile, he turned to me and said with a triumphant ring in his voice: "I know why you were humming that Russian music." "Why?" I asked. "Because my parents were Russian," he said.

All artists need appreciation of their work from other people. It was especially so with George. With him it was a very vital need—he loved it and was hungry for it the way a flower is hungry for water. His talent thrived on success.

George loved playing the piano for people and would do it at the slightest provocation. At any gathering of friends, if there was a piano in the room, George would play it. I am sure that most of his friends in thinking of George at his best, think of George at the piano. I've heard many pianists and composers play for informal gatherings, but I know of no one who did it with such genuine delight and verve. Just as the few chosen people are blessed with *joie de vivre* so was George blessed with

53

the joy of playing the piano. George at the piano was George happy. He would draw a lovely melody out of the keyboard like a golden thread, then he would play with it and juggle it, twist it and toss it around mischievously, weave it into unexpected intricate patterns, tie it in knots and untie it and hurl it into a cascade of everchanging rhythms and counterpoints. George at the piano was like a gay sorcerer celebrating his Sabbath.

He enjoyed his playing as much as his listeners did. Nor did he ever get tired of a melody. He could play *I've Got Rhythm* for the thousandth time, yet do it with such freshness and exuberance as if he had written it the night before. Through the whole period of *Porgy* rehearsals, whenever we got together for an evening of relaxation, George would get to the piano and play *Porgy and Bess* again. I remember once during rehearsals he invited me to spend a weekend with him and some friends in Long Beach. "You must come out, Rouben, to relax and forget about *Porgy and Bess* and my music for a while," he said. I couldn't go, but on Monday morning I asked Alexander Steinert, who was in the party, what did they do over the weekend at George's. Alex replied, "We played *Porgy and Bess* Saturday and Sunday—all day and all night."

George was like a child. He had a child's innocence and imagination. He could look at the same thing ever so many times and yet see it anew every time he looked at it and enjoy it. I remember once we were playing tennis at his home in Beverly Hills. This was after George and Ira had written the score for an Astaire-Rogers picture which had in it the wistful song, *No, No, You Can't Take That Away From Me.* Now, George took his tennis, as most of the things he did, close to heart. He was not a very good player—I was even worse. Still whenever he missed the ball he was

54

heartbroken—he would clutch the racket to his chest and moan, "No-o, no-o!" Once, when he missed the ball and moaned "No-o, no-o," I sang out, "You Can't Take That Away From Me!" George laughed with delight. So after that every time George missed and moaned "No-o, no-o," I came forth with a lusty "You Can't Take That Away From Me!" We did it time and again—and every time George would burst into laughter as if it had never happened before.

Also once, when we were sitting around the swimming pool in bright sunshine, George brought out his small motion-picture camera and photographed the whole company in what is called a slow "panning" shot. He was very earnest about that too. When the lens reached me, I was so amused at the concentrated expression on George's face that I broke into laughter. Later, when showing the film on the screen to his friends, as the camera reached me he would say in the darkened room, "Now I will direct Mamoulian . . . Laugh, Rouben, laugh!"—and he would time this so that right after his words I would break into inaudible laughter on the screen—after which George would laugh very lustily and very audibly. He loved this. He did it every time he ran the film. George was like a child.

Yet at times he was also like a patriarch. I would look at him and all but see a long white beard and a staff in his hand. This would usually happen whenever a group of people around him argued violently about something. George would smile and look at them as though they were little children. His face would seem to say, "You are all such lovely people and you are all a little foolish in your loud excitement. You are sweet to be so vehement and I really love you for it—but stop now—you've had enough." He was old then and wise and tolerant. A patriarch.

55

The simple gaiety of a child and the clear serenity of the old were the two extremities of George's character. In between there was much in him that was neither as simple nor as clear, nor perhaps, as happy. George did not live easily. He was a complicated, nervous product of our age. There was in him an intricate and restless combination of intellectual and emotional forces. Conflicting impulses clashed within him and played havoc. Nor was he free of complexes and inhibitions. These he always tried to analyze. To most people "Know thyself" is a vaguely-remembered line of Socrates. To George it was of vital importance. I think that to know himself was what he wanted most in life. That is why there was so much of the introvert in George. He wanted to know what he was made of and "what made it work." He searched for a solution of himself.

I am not going any further into this phase of George's character—how could I, or anyone for that matter, fathom these shadowy depths of his nature? All I can do is to indicate them because they were so much and so importantly a part of him. So inquisitive was George about himself that for the last two years of his life he was having himself psycho-analyzed. He was hoping the psycho-analyst would unravel to him his own mystery.

With all this, George had a keen and joyous sense of humor. His was not the limited sense of humor which merely loves a funny story and is able to recognize one. It was the deeper sense of noticing the amusing in everything that happens in life, around oneself and within oneself. The stories he told with affectionate amusement about people on the street, his friends, his own family, would fill a book. He kept his sense of humor even in relation to things that were of utmost importance to him. Once, during a very earnest discussion of psycho-analysis, I asked him, "Tell me, George, how much does a psycho-analyst usually charge?" George smiled

56

and answered, "He finds out how much you make and then charges you more than you can afford!" George knew how to smile and laugh.

The world will always remember George Gershwin, the composer. His music will remind them. As long as people dance and sing and play, as long as concert halls and radio remain on this earth—George Gershwin remains on this earth. He lives as a part of the world's music—is there a life more beautiful or more real?

As for those of us who knew George intimately and were his friends— George also lives on as a person. His gentle smile, his innocent spirit are with us and we think of him always—not with sorrow, but with joy and gladness, knowing within our hearts that a man like George never dies.

1938·TODD
DUNCAN

24 January 1935

DEAR MR. DUNCAN:

I received your letter and was very glad to learn how you felt about my music for *Porgy.* I appreciate your nice remarks.

As anxious as you seem to be to get hold of the music just so anxious am I to hear you sing it.

I am leaving for Florida this weekend where I begin the task of orchestrating the opera. I just finished a trio in the last scene for Porgy, Serena and Maria which I think will interest you very much.

While I am away the Theatre Guild or Mr. Wachsman will get in touch with you to do whatever ironing out there has to be done.

Before I leave I am sending two acts of the opera to my publishers and a copy will be made available to you as soon as they are printed.

With regards to you and your wife;

Yours sincerely,

GEORGE GERSHWIN.

Three years have passed since I received this letter; many things have happened. But I know that George Gershwin was sincere when he wrote these words, "Just so anxious am I to hear you sing it."

If you had ever sat near him while his music was being performed, or better yet, if you had had the good fortune to sing or play any of his music while he was present, you would have witnessed a man, all ears, moving along with the rhythms, swaying with the lilting melodies, and living so completely in the composition that you would wonder whether he had ever heard it. If your muscles have taken an extra leap with his intricate and unique rhythms; if you felt that chill down your spine when you heard the duet music in the Kittiwah scene of *Porgy and Bess* between Crown and Bess, and again in those seductive strains of the third act when Sportin' Life is imploring Bess to go to "Noo York" with him, you have experienced but a small part of what George Gershwin felt when he heard it. He loved his own music, believed in it, and was always "anxious to hear" it sung.

While *Porgy and Bess* was in rehearsal, the composer was present for an hour or two almost every day. It was then that I sensed the man's incredible enthusiasm for his own score. One day when we were in the midst of hard work in Serena's Prayer Scene, he walked in and immediately disappeared into the back of the dark theatre where he quietly took his seat. The director, Rouben Mamoulian, was working like mad with the actors setting the entrances, positions, the music and action. This is a very quiet scene, one of profound religious fervor. We singers were very tired, tired enough fortunately to set up the exact atmosphere required for the prayer. It must have been our tenth consecutive trial when I sang the following words about my Bess, "I think that maybe she gonna sleep now, a whole week gone and now she ain't no better." Serena, the pious old lady of Catfish Row, came over to me in order to offer a prayer for the sick woman, and so the prayer began.

Miss Elzy (Serena) went down on her knees as if her own mother had been ill for weeks; she felt the need of prayer. Two seconds of silence

59

intervened that seemed like hours, and presently there rose the most glorious tones and wails with accompanying amens and hallelujahs for our sick Bess that I ever hope to experience. This particular scene should have normally moved into the scene of the Street Cries, but it did not. It stopped there. The piano accompaniment ceased, every actor (and there were sixty-five of them) had come out of his rest position, sitting at the edge of his seat and R. M. was standing before us quietly moving his inevitable cigar from one side of his mouth to the other, his face lighted to sheer delight in realization, and then, George Gershwin like a ghost from the dark rows of the Guild theatre appeared before the footlights. He simply could not stand it. He knew then, that he had put down on paper accurately and truthfully something from the depth of soul of a South Carolina Negro woman who feels the need of help and carries her troubles to her God.

If on the other hand, a singer were able to inject an interesting bit of humor into his score, George Gershwin got it immediately. I had rehearsed with myself *Plenty o' Nuttin'* a hundred times, a hundred different ways, but I was still not pleased. At last, the idea clicked in my own consciousness. George Gershwin knew as well as I did when that moment came and appreciated my growth to his song's consciousness. After about ten weeks' run on Broadway, he came into my dressing room with a chuckling comment on my way of singing the words "No use complainin'." I said I would not tell him my secret, and he assured me that I had sung it exactly as he and his brother, Ira, had conceived it, and had caught precisely what he had heard some one in Charleston, S. C., express in the word "complainin'." Although I let the incident pass unnoticed then, as I was interested in getting out and home for much-needed rest, I have since heard the song many times on the radio, in concert and on recordings. I can appreciate now what George Gershwin meant. Many who sing it never get what the composer intended, nor do they sing what he has on the printed page. The simplicity, the "nuttin'," even the chuckle is always there. Try to find it yourself.

The composer was not always pleased with the performance of his music. I would not have you believe that he was. Enthusiastic and exuberant as he appeared when you did something interesting with his score, he could be equally resentful when you missed the point. How quickly he would stop you, if you had sung a wrong note; particularly, would be disturbed if you could not sense a rhythmic pattern or an offbeat pulsation which he had so carefully calculated. That would draw him to the footlights like a ball from a cannon. I recall a particular rehearsal day when an individual, whose name I do not wish to mention, sang everything wrong. The poor singer sang before the beat, after the beat, around the beat and with an occasional wrong word. Musically, he just did not function that day. The pianist hammered out the score for the singer to no avail, the musical director took his seat in sheer exasperation; R. M. moved quietly over to the wings of the theatre with an air of "Let me forget this person," and we poor singers completely lost patience and voices, from our futile singing of portions of the score over and over again. It was more than George Gershwin could bear; he paced nervously up and down the aisles of the theatre, down to the footlights again and again and finally called for his chauffeur to please take him home to his desk for his orchestrations of the Porgy score which he was doing at that time. The next day, he returned. I heard him ask "Where's Porgy?" Some one beckoned to the back of the theatre where I sat. "Todd," he said, "don't you think we'd better replace this person for the part of————?" I told him that I was certain that the individual could get the part and that I would do all I could to help. The laughable truth is that this particular part of the score has not been learned by that individual, until this very day, three years hence.

One other occasion gave George Gershwin no little concern about his score. A complete performance of the opera as written required some four and a half hours, which everybody knew was impossible. There came the day when wholesale cuts had to be made. Trouble and worry beset the composer so that R. M., the composer and the musical heads had conference after conference. The opening scene of the first act was taken out, then the Crap Game music was redone, and when at length Maria's humorous readings in the second act were taken out, all of us weakened. Then came the slashing of the thirty-eight continuous pages of Porgy's singing in the third act, and the throwing out of Porgy's big tragic aria, *The Buzzard Song.* These changes and more were finally agreed upon by all concerned, but when the suggestion that G. G.'s beloved trio in the third act (of which he had written in the letter of 1935) should be cut, it was too much for him. The trio was beautiful and the composer had embodied in it his themes previously used, weaving them into an interesting lace work of counterpoint in which he took pride and delight. He told me it was his first trio. But a portion of it too was cut when George Gershwin reluctantly agreed that it was for the best. I was told that the three, Gershwin, Mamoulian and Smallens, spent the night walking in the Boston Common discussing cuts that must be made before we reached the Alvin Theatre in New York for the premiere. Their toughest customer was George; but who could blame him?

Mr. Gershwin relived his music whether it was performed by others or whether he participated in it as soloist or accompanist. It was my good fortune to have him accompany me in his own songs under every conceivable condition; from the Atlantic to the Pacific. He accompanied me at the piano at Condé Nast's magnificent apartment and later in a little room in Harlem; we sang and played for the Dutch Treat Club in a New York down-town hotel with a hundred or more music men present, and we sang in his studio, the very top room of his penthouse apartment on Seventy-second Street where only his brother, Ira, was present. We met musically on the west coast at the Philharmonic Auditorium in Los Angeles and later at the Trocadero; back east again in the open air at the Lewisohn stadium. And in all situations, his approach to his performance was the same, the effect was the same. A performance with George Gershwin as accompanist was a transcendent experience. It commanded the attention of all alike; the intelligentsia, the so-called low brow; the rich and poor; the thousands or the one. My association with him in these performances was the same that I experience with my very fine voice-teacher and coach. I never fail to feel happy after a voice lesson and as though I can sing to the world without a single apology. George Gershwin gave me that same confident assurance, so necessary for a public performer. He was always sincere, moving and vibrant, alert to his duty toward the performance of his music. He could always set up the vibrations he desired in a room. He possessed great genius in this respect and I shall always be grateful for the lesson he taught me.

While he was firm in insisting that absolute adherence to the musical score be maintained, he was always sympathetic to any suggestion given by his singers. There was, for instance, the Sportin' Life of the New York cast who had experienced great success on the vaudeville stage and who

63

was not too particular about a musical score with symphonic accompaniment. The singer much preferred the "ad libs"; further, this individual would hold a particular note two beats on Monday night but on Tuesday night he might sustain that same note through six beats. Consequently, this very fine actor would conceive and reconceive Mr. Gershwin's score as often as he sang it. Frequently, George Gershwin's keen sense of humor would help him over what might have been a tragic moment between singer and composer, not to speak of tilts between singer and orchestral conductor.

I cannot bring to a close these memories of George Gershwin without mentioning something which he eagerly anticipated. I give to you the last letter which he wrote to me. Read for yourself. George Gershwin's wish was fulfilled.

March 16, 1937

DEAR TODD:

Just a little note to tell you what a great pleasure it was to have you come out to Los Angeles and sing at the two concerts. Your voice sounded better than ever. I'm sure you got a big kick out of receiving such a fine reception from a distinguished audience as we had.

I hope Mr. Armitage can manage to bring the entire opera out next season. He is definitely a superior impresario who does things well and I would love the West Coast to hear my opera as it was originally sung in New York.

Please extend my best wishes to Mrs. Duncan. With kind regards,

Sincerely,

GEORGE GERSHWIN.

J. ROSAMOND
1938·JOHNSON

It was in Boston at the close of the first public performance of *Porgy and Bess*. George Gershwin smiled graciously in his own inimitable manner. He had witnessed the favorite child of his brain, had heard the unanimous applause from the audience. As he stood there on the stage of the Colonial Theatre, I was amazed at the modest manner in which he received many warm and hearty congratulations. Finally, when I got a chance to grasp his hand, I whispered to him, "George, you've done it —you're the Abraham Lincoln of Negro music." The next day at rehearsal, George said to me, "Rosamond, I want to thank you for what you said last night." Well, I had christened him the "Abraham Lincoln of American Negro music," because he had, with one broad sweep clarified and removed all doubt as to the possibility of using American Negro idioms in reaching the heights of serious musical achievement.

The attention of the music world was first attracted along similar lines by the use of the old Negro spiritual *Swing Low Sweet Chariot* which can be recognized in the first movement of Dvoràk's *Symphony No. 5* (from the *New World*). Dvoràk's Symphony is one of the seven great masterpieces in the entire field of musical literature.

The next epoch in the history of distinctive American music was George Gershwin's *Rhapsody in Blue* in which the basic tonality, melodic and rhythmically, is one hundred per cent Negroid. Mr. Gershwin unhesitatingly acknowledged this fact by a delightful gesture when he autographed a copy of the work for Mr. W. C. Handy ("The Father of the Blues") as follows:

> "For Mr. Handy, whose early blue songs are the forefathers of this work."
>
> —George Gershwin, Aug. 30, 1926."

Gershwin's *Rhapsody in Blue,* whenever played in a creditable manner, is a signal for tremendous applause. The unceasing popularity of *Rhapsody in Blue* was encouraging and definitely inspired George to make extensive study of the idioms and characteristics of American folklore. With his vast and intimate knowledge of the so-called "jazz," Eastside New York ditties and other phases and styles of rendering current dance tunes, he very successfully moulded a distinctive "break-away" from the old standards in serious musical composition. In this, nevertheless, he followed the old masters, who, in their day, developed their themes through the influence of peasant songs.

Songs of the peasant in this country are the songs of the soil. Songs of the soil in America are at least ninety per cent the songs which came from the hearts and souls of the Negro—the Negro passing through his environment of slavery, freedom, the cotton field, the levee, his hours of recreation in the "dives" and barrooms along the tenderloin districts among Negroes. George Gershwin, in his thorough research, found in these Negro melodies, rhythms and idioms, unlimited food for thought and gained unparalleled inspiration. The influence of which can easily be realized in his *Porgy and Bess* folk opera.

Porgy and Bess is a monument to the cultural aims of Negro art. Intonations and intervals of the score place the opera among the most difficult ever written. Gershwin, in seeking a mode to express the peculiarities of the Negro singer, found himself inventing new musical symbols in order to notate the quarter-tone dissonances and glissandos as employed in singing the "blues." With the use of these dissonant chromatic passages, he utilized unique musical knowledge, blending them into harmonious patterns which he believed only Negro singers could give the desired result. He therefore turned a deaf ear to those who insisted that his score of *Porgy and Bess* should be sung by white vocalists with traditional operatic experience. George held to his own belief and straightway set out to make a survey of colleges, institutes and conservatories of music to find what he wanted. Among those who made auditions he found Negro artists singing Schubert, Brahms and operatic arias in their original text. His selection of Todd Duncan, as Porgy, and Anne Wiggins Brown, as Bess, and Ruby Elzy, as Serena, made history for Negroes in creating these unusually difficult operatic roles.

While Gershwin's *Porgy and Bess* may not be considered one hundred per cent Negroid as is his *Rhapsody in Blue,* yet it is quite convincing that at least eighty per cent of its musical idioms are. The remaining twenty per cent might be contributed to twists and turns characteristic of the American Indian with a slight persuasion of cowboy ditties and mountain airs—which are American and by the process of a melting-pot of these musical idioms it served its purpose to enhance the valuation of his *Porgy and Bess* folk opera into an original musical work, standardizing a distinctively American formula for present-day composers of serious music.

Composers may vary from the Gershwin treatment finding other media of musical expression in the same manner as the different styles and forms of European standards vary, but unless their melodic intervals and rhythmic idioms are based on the wealth of American folklore, as were George Gershwin's, such a work, internationally, would have a very doubtful impression or conviction as a distinctive work along the lines of establishing a recognized School of American Music.

George Gershwin, in this respect, has sounded the most effective call of awakening to the culture and development of American idioms, based solely on the folklore of America since Anton Dvoràk's Symphony *From the New World.*

Among the best composers of America, Victor Herbert stands eminently as a prolific writer of melodic songs and serious works as well. His compositions, however, were of a different type than those of Gershwin. Herbert in this work invariably showed the influence of an Irish lilt, while George Gershwin bent down into native soil and based his recent works on the American folk songs of a lowly people.

Victor Herbert was beloved and still lives in the fondest memories of all musical America as a tower of strength in paving the way for recognition of American composers, and in doing so he also had a timely vision along another line exceedingly helpful to his fellow-brethren of the music world. The immortal soul of Victor Herbert unquestionably rejoices for the success and stimulating activities of The American Society of Composers, Authors and Publishers (A.S.C.A.P.). This master composer loved and cherished the art of giving his marvelous melodies to the music-loving world, but at the very height of his musical career he devoted practically (and with an unselfish motive) all of his time and energy to making the A.S.C.A.P. the "Rock of Ages" for writers of today and "yesterdays." Who knows, perhaps our beloved George Gershwin, without the workings of A. S. C. A. P.'s effectiveness, may never have given to America such a great work as his musical setting to *Porgy and Bess* and this fact would have proven a great loss to America in her journey by ways and means of acquiring universal recognition in the world of music with a standard of distinctiveness in a school of music all her own.

The musical influence of George Gershwin's *Porgy and Bess* will live through the ages and transition of musical vogues as a fountain of inspiration to writers. Some may differ at great length from his unusual style, but nevertheless the example and magnitude of this young man's musical exposition and development of folklore, emanating from street cries, blues and plantation songs of the Negro, will prove itself a beacon light to those who are brave enough to stray from the "web-worn" standards of the great masters of Europe.

Should such a process be heeded through the influence of Dvoràk's Symphony *From the New World*, George Gershwin's *Rhapsody in Blue* and his immortal contribution of *Porgy and Bess,* distinctive American music in the serious forms of the symphony and grand opera will rightfully be acclaimed.

George Gershwin was an incessant worker. Those who knew him personally may recall his manner in moments at "parties." At all times he was gloriously happy at the piano, playing many of his songs—ofttimes crooning them in his own delightful style—never tiring, always willing to please his listeners who invariably revelled in the glow and warmth of his inspiring personality. On such occasions, if George were not at the piano, you would find him in some far corner and yet, while remaining as one of the group, he was continually thinking, thinking, always thinking.

It was only through the kindly expression of his eyes and the modest yet captivating smile which sent out the exquisite pleasure he felt in being among friends. One might imagine George Gershwin at a ball game, tennis, boxing match, or riding on a train continually seeking the rhythm of each movement. It is said that he caught the rhythm for his famous song *Swanee* while riding a-top a New York City bus along Riverside Drive.

It seems regrettable that young composers like Samuel Coleridge-Taylor, European, born of African and English parentage—well schooled in the precepts of English musical culture, yet always sounding the distinctive note of his African heritage transplanted in his setting of *Hiawatha,* an American legend by the American poet Longfellow—and George Gershwin, American, born of Jewish-Russian parentage—well tutored in the classics of European standards of music as a pianist, saturated with the impressions of American idioms in his *Rhapsody in Blue* should die in their youth; yet it is quite gratifying to know that they shall never be forgotten. Coleridge-Taylor's *Hiawatha* will live forever—George Gershwin's *Rhapsody in Blue,* his *Porgy and Bess* will never die.

George Gershwin worked hard during his career. Within the short period of ten years he contributed to his library of original compositions a vast amount of material that would possibly have taken the average musical genius twenty-five years or more to complete. He was an ardent student, even in his last moment, never ceasing, a genius with an innate vision who had the courage to carry on until the final curtain lowered.

Composers and critics alike are guided largely by their own opinions and inspirations. It is not then strange that George Gershwin's music evoked varied and sundry criticisms. About twenty per cent of America's

70

critics were somewhat derogatory in their remarks pertaining musically to the religious fervor of the Negro in *Porgy and Bess,* while eighty per cent of Gershwin's critics seemed to grasp his sincere spirit of conveying the Negro's religious fervor, especially for operatic effect, by the use of counterpoint and fugue. This, to my mind, was the noble thing to do rather than the use of the Negro spiritual in its traditional form.

Perhaps my overwhelming reverence for George Gershwin may be prompted by a somewhat personal or selfish motive. Be that as it may— it is exceedingly gratifying to me that he has set the "key-stone" of a structure, holding together the idioms and characteristics of the Negro in the Modern School of American Music.

> "Go back, Musical Youth of America,
> Back to the songs of a lowly people!
> Hold fast their idioms,
> Nourish—and rock them
> In the Cradle of American Music."

1935·GEORGE GERSHWIN

Since the opening of *Porgy and Bess* I have been asked frequently why it is called a folk opera. The explanation is a simple one. *Porgy and Bess* is a folk tale. Its people naturally would sing folk music. When I first began work on the music I decided against the use of original folk material because I wanted the music to be all of one piece. Therefore I wrote my own spirituals and folksongs. But they are still folk music—and therefore, being in operatic form, *Porgy and Bess* becomes a folk opera.

However, because *Porgy and Bess* deals with Negro life in America it brings to the operatic form elements that have never before appeared in opera and I have adapted my method to utilize the drama, the humor, the superstition, the religious fervor, the dancing and the irrepressible high spirits of the race. If, in doing this, I have created a new form, which combines opera with theatre, this new form has come quite naturally out of the material.

The reason I did not submit this work to the usual sponsors of opera in America was that I hoped to have developed something in American music that would appeal to the many rather than to the cultured few.

It was my idea that opera should be entertaining—that it should contain all the elements of entertainment. Therefore, when I chose *Porgy and Bess,* a tale of Charleston Negroes, for a subject, I made sure that it would enable me to write light as well as serious music and that it would enable me to include humor as well as tragedy—in fact, all of the elements of entertainment for the eye as well as the ear, because the Negroes, as a race, have all these qualities inherent in them. They are ideal for my purpose because they express themselves not only by the spoken word but quite naturally by song and dance.

Humor is an important part of American life, and an American opera without humor could not possibly run the gamut of American expression. In *Porgy and Bess* there are ample opportunities for humorous songs and dances. This humor is natural humor—not "gags" superimposed upon the story but humor flowing from the story itself.

For instance, the character of Sportin' Life, instead of being a sinister dope-peddler, is a humorous, dancing villain, who is likable and believable and at the same time evil. We were fortunate in finding for that rôle a young man whose abilities suit it perfectly, John W. Bubbles, or, as he is known to followers of vaudeville, just plain Bubbles, of Buck and Bubbles. We were equally fortunate in finding Todd Duncan for the rôle of Porgy and Anne Brown for the rôle of Bess, both of whom give to the score intense dramatic value. We were able to find these people because what we wanted from them lies in their race. And thus it lies in our story of their race. Many people questioned my choice of a vaudeville performer for an operatic rôle but on the opening night they cheered Bubbles.

We were fortunate, too, in being able to lure Rouben Mamoulian, a great director, back from Hollywood to stage the production. It was Mr. Mamoulian who staged the original production of *Porgy* as a play. He knew all of its value. What was even more valuable, he knew opera as well as he knew the theatre and he was able to bring his knowledge of both to this new form. In my opinion, he has left nothing to be desired

73

in the direction. To match the stage in the pit we obtained Alexander Smallens, who has directed the Philadelphia and Philharmonic Symphony Orchestras and who has conducted more than 150 operas and who has been invaluable to us.

I chose the form I have used for *Porgy and Bess* because I believe that music lives only when it is in serious form. When I wrote the *Rhapsody in Blue* I took "blues" and put them in a larger and more serious form. That was twelve years ago and the *Rhapsody in Blue* is still very much alive, whereas if I had taken the same themes and put them in songs they would have been gone years ago.

No story could have been more ideal for the serious form I needed than *Porgy and Bess.* First of all, it is American, and I believe that American music should be based on American material. I felt when I read *Porgy* in novel form that it had 100 per cent dramatic intensity in addition to humor. It was then that I wrote to DuBose Heyward suggesting that we make an opera of it.

My feelings about it, gained from that first reading of the novel, were confirmed when it was produced as a play, for audiences crowded the theatre where it played for two years. Mr. Heyward and I, in our collaboration on *Porgy and Bess,* have attempted to heighten the emotional values of the story without losing any of its original quality. I have written my music to be an integral part of that story.

It is true that I have written songs for *Porgy and Bess.* I am not ashamed of writing songs at any time so long as they are good songs. In *Porgy and Bess* I realized I was writing an opera for the theatre and without songs it could be neither of the theatre nor entertaining, from my viewpoint.

But songs are entirely within the operatic tradition. Many of the most successful operas of the past have had songs. Nearly all of Verdi's operas contain what are known as "song hits." *Carmen* is almost a collection of song hits. And what about *The Last Rose of Summer,* perhaps one of the most widely known songs of the generation? How many of those who sing it know that it is from an opera?

Of course, the songs in *Porgy and Bess* are only a part of the whole. The recitative I have tried to make as close to the Negro inflection in speech as possible, and I believe my song-writing apprenticeship has served invaluably in this respect, because the song writers of America have the best conception of how to set words to music so that the music gives added expression to the words. I have used sustained symphonic music to unify entire scenes, and I prepared myself for that task by further study in counterpoint and modern harmony.

In the lyrics for *Porgy and Bess* I believe that Mr. Heyward and my brother, Ira, have achieved a fine synchronization of diversified moods— Mr. Heyward writing most of the native material and Ira doing most of the sophisticated songs. To demonstrate the range of mood their task covers, let me cite a few examples.

There is the prayer in the storm scene written by Mr. Heyward:

> Oh, de Lawd shake de Heavens an' de Lawd rock de groun',
> An' where you goin' stand, my brudder an' my sister,
> When de sky come a-tumblin' down.
>
> Oh, de sun goin' to rise in de wes'
> An' de moon goin' to set in de sea
> An' de stars goin' to bow befo' my Lawd,
> Bow down befo' my Lawd,
> Who died on Calvarie.

And in contrast there is Ira's song for Sportin' Life in the picnic scene:

> It ain't necessarily so,
> It ain't necessarily so,
> De t'ings dat yo' li'ble
> To read in de Bible,
> It ain't necessarily so.
>
> Li'l David was small, but oh my!
> Li'l David was small, but oh my!
> He fought big Goliath
> Who lay down an' dieth.
> Li'l David was small, but oh my!

Then there is Mr. Heyward's lullaby that opens the opera:

> Summer time, an' the livin' is easy,
>   Fish are jumpin', an' the cotton is high.
> Oh, yo' daddy's rich an' yo' ma is good-lookin',
>   So hush, little baby, don't yo' cry.
>
> One of these mornin's you goin' to rise up singin',
>   Then you'll spread yo' wings an' you'll take the sky.
> But 'til that mornin' there's a nothin' can harm you
>   With Daddy an' Mammy standin' by.

And, again, Ira's song for Sportin' Life in the last act:

> There's a boat dat's leavin' soon for New York.
>   Come wid me, dat's where we belong, sister.
> You an' me kin live dat high life in New York.
>   Come wid me, dere you can't go wrong, sister.
>
> I'll buy you de swellest mansion
>   Up on upper Fi'th Avenue,
> An' through Harlem we'll go struttin',
>   We'll go a-struttin',
> An' dere'll be nuttin'
>   Too good for you.

76

All of these are, I believe, lines that come naturally from the Negro. They make for folk music. Thus *Porgy and Bess* becomes a folk opera—opera for the theatre, with drama, humor, song and dance.

IRVING
May 16, 1938 · BERLIN

I could speak of a Whiteman rehearsal
At the old Palais Royal when Paul
Played the "Rhapsody" that lifted Gershwin
From the "Alley" to Carnegie Hall.
I could dwell on the talent that placed him
In the class where he justly belongs,
But this verse is a song-writer's tribute
To a man who wrote wonderful songs.

His were tunes that had more than just rhythm,
For just rhythm will soon gather "corn,"
And those melodies written by Gershwin
Are as fresh now as when they were born.
As a writer of serious music,
He could dream for a while in the stars,
And step down from the heights of Grand Opera
To a chorus of thirty-two bars.

78

And this morning's Variety tells me

That the last song he wrote is a hit,

It's on top in the list of best sellers,

And the air-waves are ringing with it.

It remains with the dozens of others,

Though the man who composed them is gone;

For a song-writer's job may be ended,

But his melodies linger on.

GEORGE GERSHWIN

PORTRAIT BY ISAMU NOGUCHI

ORCHESTRAL REHEARSAL

SERGE KOUSSEVITZKY AND GEORGE GERSHWIN TAKEN IN BOSTON

PHILHARMONIC ORCHESTRA OF LOS ANGELES, FEBRUARY, 1937

GEORGE GERSHWIN AND IRVING BERLIN, A TIME EXPOSURE TAKEN BY GEORGE GERSHWIN

BEVERLY HILLS, JANUARY, 1937

GEORGE GERSHWIN AND JEROME KERN

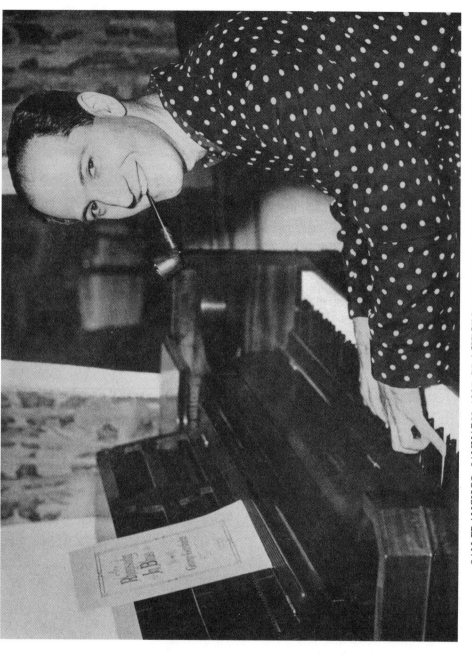

SAN FRANCISCO, JANUARY, 1937, PRACTICING FOR THE CONCERTS WITH MONTEUX AND THE SAN FRANCISCO SYMPHONY

BEVERLY HILLS . . . COLLABORATING ON *DAMSEL IN DISTRESS* WITH IRA

FRED ASTAIRE, GEORGE AND IRA REHEARSAL, *SHALL WE DANCE*

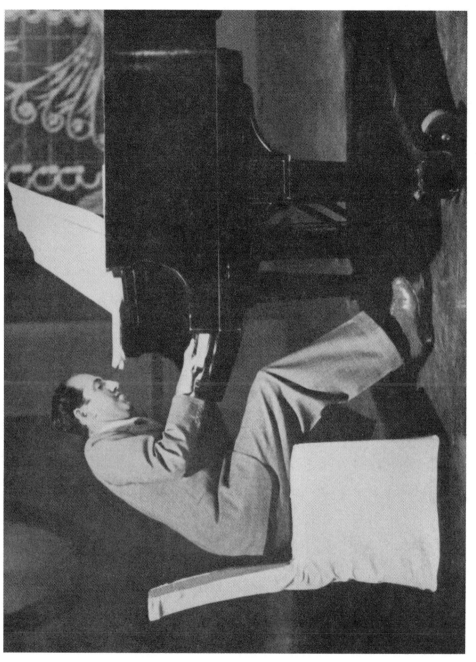

GEORGE GERSHWIN, A CANDID CAMERA PHOTOGRAPH TAKEN AT THE RKO STUDIOS LATE IN JUNE, 1937, POSSIBLY THE LAST PHOTOGRAPH EVER TAKEN OF THE COMPOSER

1938·ARNOLD SCHOENBERG

Many musicians do not consider George Gershwin a serious composer. But they should understand that, serious or not, he is a composer—that is, a man who lives in music and expresses everything, serious or not, sound or superficial, by means of music, because it is his native language. There are a number of composers, serious (as they believe) or not (as I know), who learned to add notes together. But they are only serious on account of a perfect lack of humor and soul.

It seems to me that this difference alone is sufficient to justify calling the one a composer, but the other none. An artist is to me like an apple tree: When his time comes, whether he wants it or not, he bursts into bloom and starts to produce apples. And as an apple tree neither knows nor asks about the value experts of the market will attribute to its product, so a real composer does not ask whether his products will please the experts of serious arts. He only feels he has to say something; and says it.

It seems to me beyond doubt that Gershwin was an innovator. What he has done with rhythm, harmony and melody is not merely style. It is fundamentally different from the mannerism of many a serious composer. Such mannerism is based on artificial presumptions, which are gained by speculation and are conclusions drawn from the fashions and aims current among contemporary composers at certain times. Such a style is a superficial union of devices applied to a minimum of idea, without any inner

97

reason or cause. Such music could be taken to pieces and put together in a different way, and the result would be the same nothingness expressed by another mannerism. One could not do this with Gershwin's music. His melodies are not products of a combination, nor of a mechanical union, but they are units and could therefore not be taken to pieces. Melody, harmony and rhythm are not welded together, but cast. I do not know it, but I imagine, he improvised them on the piano. Perhaps he gave them later the finishing touch; perhaps he spent much time to go over them again and again—I do not know. But the impression is that of an improvisation with all the merits and shortcomings appertaining to this kind of production. Their effect in this regard might be compared to that of an oration which might disappoint you when you read and examine it as with a magnifying glass—you miss what touched you so much, when you were overwhelmed by the charm of the orator's personality. One has probably to add something of one's own to reëstablish the first effect. But it is always that way with art—you get from a work about as much as you are able to give to it yourself.

I do not speak here as a musical theorist, nor am I a critic, and hence I am not forced to say whether history will consider Gershwin a kind of Johann Strauss or Debussy, Offenbach or Brahms, Lehar or Puccini.

But I know he is an artist and a composer; he expressed musical ideas; and they were new—as is the way in which he expressed them.

LOUIS
1938·DANZ

It has so often been said. It may therefore seem somewhat trite to say again that Art is the reflection of its time. Nevertheless, there is a most profound significance in this statement, and especially in music, the significance has been overlooked. The music critic usually views everything from his one personal standpoint. In so doing he is very apt to miss some vital creative accomplishment which is only visible from some other viewpoint. The least the critic can do is to detach himself from any viewpoint and survey the field not as a player, but merely as a very interested spectator, and just as there may be more than one viewpoint, there may many times be more than one channel of creative expression.

For instance, the critic who can see George Gershwin usually cannot see Arnold Schoenberg, and then, of course, the critic who appreciates Schoenberg cannot see Gershwin. Now in a tennis game, why does the umpire stand at the net? Why should he not stand at the right or the left end of the court? The answer is obvious. He is an umpire and not a player. In like manner one should, in appraising any creative work, stand at the net. When the critic stands at the net he can readily see the viewpoint of the players without blinding himself with his own.

It is in this way that the importance of Gershwin is understood. In the history of the music which has been composed in America, the names of Arnold Schoenberg and George Gershwin may well be linked together.

In these two creative geniuses we have the fullest expression of today. Neither one nor the other could play from both sides of the net, but both play famously from the side of their choosing.

The fact that I find it logical to link these names together when they appear to be poles apart, is easily explained. Schoenberg expresses to the utmost the structure of music as it stands in the modern world. He expresses this structure through his music. Gershwin, on the other hand, expresses to the fullest the structure of contemporary society. He expresses this structure through his music. Which is the most vital, which the most important, is an unanswerable question.

I thoroughly appreciate the grandeur of a Schoenberg quartette. I know the quartettes both structurally and emotionally. But this cannot dim my appreciation for the music of George Gershwin. The critic who does not stand at the net and watch the balls go over, but who takes a place to one side, may point out what he would call Gershwin's short-comings. He might say that the music is over-sweet, that the phrases are too short, that the whole lacks continuity, that the recitative is stilted, that there is too much repetition and so on. But I say, these are not defects inherent in the music, these are the defects of modern society. Gershwin holds the mirror of music to the face of society. If we are sweet, we are apt to be over-sweet. Our phrases are short, the sharp blast of the auto horn is a dominant symbol of today. And we lack continuity. Though our slang is stilted, it is powerfully expressive. And further, repetition is ours by right of conquest. It makes our slogans effective.

On the other hand, the critic playing from the other end of the net, would say that the music of Arnold Schoenberg is cold, restless, unemotional and artificial; in fact, it is not music, it is merely arithmetic.

100

It is true that Arnold Schoenberg is not concerned with modern society. His concern is wholly with the formal structure of music as it develops, apart from its environment. To him music is an organism with the unalienable right to live in the abstract. Schoenberg stands alone, apart from the people.

To the critic standing at the net, Schoenberg towers like a mountain peak up which only the most daring would venture. There he stands in formal emotionality—the condensation of the history of pure music. While down below in the warm valleys the people listen to Gershwin. Schoenberg is so gigantic that they cannot get him into their houses. But Gershwin is so persuasive that his entrance even if uninvited, seems unobtrusive and natural—never formal, but warm like a hand-shake.

And what critic, standing at the net, would dare say which of these two men is the most vital? Both are expressive of the times—the one is the organic outcome of the growth of structure, as a thing in itself; the other is an expressive member of society through whom the history of the people finds an outlet. Let us then be satisfied to enjoy the game, to watch the balls as they fly over the net—but let us not try to follow the balls to see where they light. In this subtle game of music, the field is much too vast and the eyes of man grow dim with distances.

ALBERT HEINK
1938·SENDREY

I was sitting in my bath, reading the *Hollywood Reporter,* when Arnold Schoenberg phoned.

"How about some tennis today?" he queried.

"I'd like nothing better," says I.

"Then be at Gershwin's house in an hour. Bis dahin, auf Wiedersehen."

It was too late to think of an excuse. My game, although it fulfilled its purpose with the average opponent, was no match for the lean and wiry "Blue Rhapsodist," and I had previously promised George, that before venturing out on his court again, I would have fortified myself with lessons from Vines or Budge. For Gershwin was something of a dandy, and just as he liked his music to be better groomed, more smartly turned out, than the music of other men, so he liked his game to be impeccable; and here he expected the same from his opponent.

The day was perfect, just as the California Tourist Bureau expects it to be; the sky turquoise blue, edged with a tinge of white, the air clear and already trembling with midday heat. A slight breeze blew in from the hills that had caressed orange blossoms, and bore their sweet and yet heavy fragrance.

The hour was peace over that creamy-white house on Roxbury Drive. The only sounds were the buzzing of insects over the pool, and the rhythmic patter of balls on the court somewhere behind. A breath later I beheld a memorable and spectacular sight.

There they were, separated by a mere net, perhaps the two greatest and certainly the most discussed musicians of this decade. On one side the younger one who had succeeded in making a respectable woman out of that little hussy, Jazz; whose music was written in a spirit of modest grati- tude to those masters who had cleared the ground on which his great talent enabled him to build; who had taken the common barber-shop chord and transfigured it into melodies of rare beauty, into a ballad that has never been surpassed in simplicity of line and elegance of structure, the immor- tal *Man I Love*; who has elevated this inconspicuous minor seventh sitting on a major triad into the heights of everlasting music, making it his very own characteristic, the earmark of American music, which generations after us will associate with him as clearly as we do the chord of the major ninth with Debussy, the flattened sixth with Brahms, the sliding semi- tonic bass with Delius.

On the other side of that separating net the older man, agile, small of stature but immense of mind, who is beating new paths for music through the wilderness of the unknown, over which we are as yet unable to follow him; whose conception of music is abstract and essentially austere, whose emotional purport remains closely united to the working of the intellect, whose so-called dissonance is deeply concerned with consonance, and in strict accordance to the principles of classical architecture.

There they were, those two contrasting giants of modern music, George Gershwin and Arnold Schoenberg, united in one common thought to make a little ball scale the top of a net, as though nothing else mattered. Let short-sighted humanity sneer at dissonance . . . love-fifteen . . . let them call the *Rhapsody in Blue* a mere fad . . . fifteen-all . . . let them walk out pulling grimaces and holding their ears . . . thirty-fifteen . . . let them say: once Tin Pan Alley, always Tin Pan Alley . . . forty-fifteen . . . so Boris Morros thinks *Verklaerte Nacht* would make a swell picture score? . . . forty-thirty . . . let them speak of *Porgy and Bess* as a musical dwarf beside a literary Goliath, if it makes them happy . . . game and set, 6:2.

"Hello, Al, glad to see you—do you mind waiting until Mr. Schoenberg has a chance to take his revenge? Thanks, get yourself a drink, they are in the cooler beside the pool, then come over and watch a real match. By the way, has Budge improved your game any?"

I return, sucking something wet and cold through a straw. Already George has taken another game in storm from the unsuspecting little Meister.

"It ain't fair, George!" I protest meekly on Schoenberg's behalf.

But Gershwin is playing an unforgiving game, with relentless hard drives, chasing the little man about the court with well-placed shots. I seem to detect a glint of humor in his eye, and a faint smile playing about his lips. Schoenberg is now doing all he can to return sleek volleys and drives, and I see the reason why. Wonderful showman that he is, George is playing to an audience, if only to a one-man audience, but an audience, nevertheless. And he finds in admiration and praise a stimulant, whether his music is the object of this admiration, or merely a game he happens to indulge in. Here he is the exact opposite of his elder opponent, who has learned to shut his mind against public opinion, knowing it was not ready yet to comprehend what he is achieving, and also realizing that any laudatory tribute would be outweighed by adverse criticism, often hostile disparagement.

104

Deuce—advantage—game. The score is two against the little Meister, yet he remains unperturbed, determined to have his "revanche." George is now playing with a rhythmic stride which contains a movement unconscious of itself, a thing of great beauty, nonchalance combined with ease. His backhands and drives are almost musical, for is not music rhythm and harmony welded into one, melody and counterpoint? Verily, that's what it was: counterpoint! The perfect description I had felt and yet had been unable to formulate! Obviously his timing was perfect, harmonious, but underneath it there existed the very same linear rules which determine his kingdom of music—counterpoint indeed.

Thirty-all . . . thirty-forty . . . game. Things look bad for Schoenberg —George has taken three games in a row.

Gershwin's fundamental weakness was that he tried to make mere harmony do too much. He was obsessed by certain "pretty" chords, augmented ninths, chromatically altered thirteenths, to use the convenient labels. He was drugged by them into forgetfulness of the great truth that counterpoint is the vital and dynamic element of music, not harmony. Now he is aware of the fact that he is opposing the man who is perhaps the greatest contrapuntist the world has produced, with the exception of Bach and Reger. George does not realize, however, that he is defeating this contrapuntal giant opposite him because in this game rôles are reversed: He, Gershwin, expresses linear counterpoint in his strokes, whereas Schoenberg concentrates on mere harmony, the safe return of a ball, the more than physical aspect of reaching a well-placed drive in the far corner of his side; he no longer places his returns, while George is more careful than ever to achieve clarity of his intentions.

George is serving. A nonchalant wallop—how well he knows that his footwork is just right—the little man crouched low on the opposite side leaps into action, almost too eager, like a bass tuba bursting into a preceding pianissimo too soon—before he even hits the ball, his young opponent moves forward in a slightly diagonal line, right into the on-coming ball. He returns it into the left-hand corner, thus prismatically breaking its flight—this throws Schoenberg off weight, but he manages to reach that corner somehow . . . a faulty backhand (instinctively I have to think of parallel fifths and "Leittonverdopplung," the curse of a com-poser's apprenticeship—and how quickly Schoenberg can detect *them* in an otherwise perfect score!) George took that backhand in mid-air—a fast volley with a triumphant twist of his wrist (how perfectly pianistic that was—no one could have done it more musically: Bach on the tennis court!) and fifteen-love.

Service from the left—Schoenberg returns with a backhand—this time his stroke had freedom and continuity, a metre sharply defined; it was a perfect introduction to a melodic phrase, now let us watch the de-velopment. George takes three steps to his right, a splendid forehand straight across the court into the diametrical corner is the result, but Schoenberg sees it coming and is already in line with the ball. George's development had been tactical rather than strategic counterpoint. The little man returns it straight along the side-line, dolcissimo, and George has quite a time reaching it near the net . . . I wonder whether his counter-point will work . . . yes, perfect; his stroke formed as he approached the ball from the right, an immaculate backhand. Here is his chance to send the ball across almost parallel to the net, forever out of his opponent's reach, but no . . . he chooses to be chivalrous, endearing trait in him—and he gives Schoenberg an even chance. This is the gradual unfoldment of a dominant idea working its way towards completion. The little Meister seizes his chance, but his ball goes out . . . thirty-love.

Art, I muse, as I watch these two genii in action, is of various kinds. There are men to whom truth is ultimate beauty, and men to whom beauty is ultimate truth, or in other words, those for whom their art is above all an interpretation of life, and those others for whom it constitutes an escape from it, a realistic dream world of their own. There are artists classical and artists romantic, composers academic and composers revolutionary, creators of the real and creators of the fantastic. It would be presumptuous to assign to any one of these types a higher or lower rank than another on the ground that the type he represents is of greater or of less value, but we can more easily indicate the measure of his achievement as a representative of that class not only by the conventions which he has established, but more so by those which he has broken down. Verdicts which we may pass today on both Gershwin and Schoenberg will be revised in fifty years from now, when the future will have given posterity the full key to their work, rendered clear what still remains enigmatic in them to us, and revealed in the light of precursors those two composers whom at present many consider retrogressive and insignificant where the younger is concerned, on account of his love for pure American folklore and on account of the sincerity and simplicity of his expression; ultra-revolutionary the other, and rebel against all that is holy and sacred in music, because of his love for pure form and because of the austerity of his idiom. Apparent paralogism, but the bitter truth.

Verdicts may be revised, I mused further, but on this tennis court were the two men who had done most for music since Richard Strauss launched the tone-poem into the torrent of Wagnerian drama and Beethovenian symphony, and since Ravel evolved instrumentation into orchestration, instrumental sound into radiant tone-color. Gershwin will be remembered for all time as the man who established the conventions on which American music will rise and flourish; Schoenberg as the pioneer who was content with breaking down the heavy romanticism of the nineteenth century, with all its portentous emotions and its mythological swamps, so we youngsters and the ones after us can find light and air in our music, lofty aspirations, free from sham pretensions and false egoism.

Thirty-fifteen. George, probably blinded by the midday sun, had served a double-fault. He had tried to hit the ball without looking up—isn't that an attempt to make mere harmony do too much? Mind you, I am not blaming that double-fault on his counterpoint altogether—I suppose the sun had something to do with it, too.

Service from the left—ah, a perfect parabola from the center of his racket to the fringe of a chalk line. Schoenberg had lulled himself in the security of that last double-fault, perhaps expecting another such generosity of fate—he now jumps into action too suddenly and his return lacks all rhythm, melody, harmony, to say nothing of counterpoint. It is a choppy little attempt at a stroke, but somehow the ball makes up its mind to reach the top of the net, pauses there a moment, then tumbles over lazily. Gershwin takes two enormous strides forward—another, but in vain, that little rascal of a ball never even bounces. Then laughter—the little man is holding his sides with uncontrollable mirth, can scarcely mutter an apology for the rude behavior of this little rubber imp. George just utters a broad, sunny smile, shaking his head incredulously at so much luck.

And I, silent observer, mean to detect a faint irony in this injustice of fate, a symbolic occurrence. The movement of this ball, animated by a perfect stroke, is a trend of musical creation, with themes inherently noble, sweeping along a high plane of thought, comparable to Gershwin's lifework. It is intercepted, and returned full of short-windedness where there was strength of wing, harmonic shortcomings where it possessed freedom, contrapuntal incoherence where there was ethereal lightness. And this second ball clears the net, just as the first had done, but there is nothing noble about it, nothing free, yet according to the rules of the game it is accepted and found good, thus vanquishing its master who had given it soul and being, giving victory to the other who had given it nothing. This, it seemed to me, takes place as Gershwin's music, noble and free, reaches all those whom the strength of its message makes satellites to his idiom, planets around a great stellar body. And as many of them will assert: What did Gershwin say in his music, that I am not saying? I can almost hear this small rubber ball exclaim: well, I went over, didn't I?

Thirty-all. The sun burns down onto the court, and I suck frantically through my straw. As I reach the bottom, a faint bubbling, gargling noise emerges from my bottle—George, about to serve again, looks over, visibly irritated at this interruption. I smile an apology somewhat stupidly, but already this incident has made its impression on his service, which is erratic and lands in the net. Could it be that George mistook this accidental bubbling for an uncouth sign of disapproval, or sardonic innuendo, commonly termed "raspberry," done on purpose?

We have stated that Gershwin was something of a dandy and a showman, both in the cool, transcendent quality of his intellect, in his knowledge of what he could do, and his refusal to attempt what he could not. His greatest trait of showmanship was his reluctance to take himself too seriously, no matter how seriously he was taken by the judges of his work. But, in order to create pure and poetic music, greater and better works of art, he needed praise and admiration like a flower needs sunshine and rain —banal image but irrefutable fact—and it is the opinion of some that had his *Rhapsody* not been the unprecedented success it was, he would never again have attempted anything in the realm of serious music, and his Preludes, his *Concerto in F,* his *An American in Paris,* and, of course, *Porgy and Bess,* would never have been written.

He had been playing to the grandstand, and he had honored me in letting me be his grandstand audience. Now I had repaid him with what he feared most, for the sake of his inspiration, and yet always pretended to care nothing about: taunting disapprobation, sarcastic criticism. It was to him as though an entire tribune filled with people had voiced their disrespectful opinion—his grandstand collapsed, likewise his game.

There was nothing I could do but feel utterly self-conscious. The score was now thirty-forty, in Mr. Schoenberg's favor.

George serves again. Some of his poise has left him, and been replaced by a grim determination to win despite his audience, against the odds. He is taut where he was relaxed before, nervous where he was nonchalant. His opponent on the contrary seems gay and pepped up by this sudden streak of good fortune. He fairly pounces upon the ball in mid-air, places it well out of George's reach—splendid counterpoint, I reflect—George has to run far to get it, four steps to the right—why, that was one more than he needed, his right foot is forward as his forehand drive comes through— he is off balance (parallel fifths again, and "Leittonverdopplung," I cannot help thinking) still, the ball returns meekly to Schoenberg, almost with an apology on its felty lips for coming back at all in such a manner.

Yet the little Meister pays no attention to that, he hits it vigorously in the face, the imp gives an audible plop as he changes direction once more toward his youthful master . . .

There are only a privileged few who have seen George Gershwin at work. I am not saying I have, and I am not saying I haven't. I would not know. For his work has something so "spielerisches," such an easy and natural flow of inspiration, that one never for one moment has the feeling he is begetting an opus with the labor-pains the average composer suffers. This complete absence of labor-pains (may I be forgiven the use of this word in connection with Terpsichore's art) explains to some extent the fact that when he arrives at an impasse, a point from which even his musical craftsmanship does not allow him to disentangle himself, perhaps harmonically, perhaps thematically, he will, in a quick outburst of temperament combined with sound reasoning throw aside the idea in its entirety, not persevere, nor ask guidance from some adviser, be it a Grofé or a Dr. Szirmay. He will make a new start, discarding the material which has been the cause of this dead end, and here is the reason why his music is fresh and unconstrained, has form as well as structure, method as well as direction.

When George saw this ball coming toward him, he realized perhaps that he was in just such an impasse—a contrapuntal entanglement, a harmonic mess, a rhythmic disorganization. With one last "don't give a damn" slam he attacked the ball, aiming it right into the net. But in that last stroke he had regained all his poise, all his balance, all his harmonious timing, he was once again the master of counterpoint, rhythm, and perfect form. His aim had been good—he unloosened a faint smile when the victim of his temper landed with one last painful plop in the net.

| | |

And then, without the least trace of rancor toward his straw-sucking audience which had spoiled his game, he said, just what he would have said when getting up from his piano after having torn up an embryonic idea, some incompleted line of musical expression:

"We'll continue it later—now let's have some lunch."

1938 · SERGE KOUSSEVITZKY

It was in a private home of mutual friends that I first met George Gershwin. He was known to me by name and his rapidly growing reputation on both continents. But not that alone attracted me to this young American of barely twenty. There was something infinitely simple, unassuming, radiantly light and easy-going about him; something that evoked an impression almost of unreality.

I remember that first impression clearly. It was strengthened in later years, and I wondered again and again at the God-given radiance, simplicity and ease of his whole being, which one could hardly believe possible in real life and which shone through his extraordinary musical gifts. I saw George in many a different light and surrounding; yet his personality remained as unobstructed and luminous as on that first occasion.

I recall him at the piano in a concert hall. Who ever heard Gershwin in a performance of his *Rhapsody in Blue* shall not forget the experience. The sweeping brilliance, virtuosity and rhythmic precision of his playing were incredible; his perfect poise and ease beyond belief; his dynamic influence on the orchestra and on the audience electrifying.

Again I recall him at the piano at a small friendly gathering, singing or rather reciting his own songs with his inimitable wit and intonation, that shed irresistible laughter and gaiety upon his listeners. As I watched him there, obviously the soul of the evening and as obviously unconscious

113

of it, I caught myself thinking, as if in a dream-state, that this was a delusion, the enchantment of this extraordinary being too great to be real.

I see him in the orchestra pit conducting one of his musical comedies, swinging the baton with the lightness and authority of an experienced conductor, and the orchestra played for him with enthusiasm. It was the first time he had ever conducted or held a baton in his hand.

To speak of George Gershwin the composer, is to approach the real, the essential part of his being. Like a rare flower which blossoms forth once in a long while, Gershwin represents a singularly original and rare phenomenon. Like a flower, his life was short-lived, but the blossom of his soul has, is and will be an inspiration to many a renowned composer of our day and of days to come. The voice of his music spread far beyond his country; it is heard overseas. To understand the nature of his gift and his mission, is to realize that Gershwin composed as a bird sings, because it is natural, it is inborn, it is part of its being. His, was an elementary source whch sprang from the soil. His richly endowed nature absorbed and crystallized the essence of American *lore* and poured it out into melody and rhythm with all the spontaneity, originality and dynamic strength which were his own . . .

Unassuming, never thinking of himself as an "immortal," George Gershwin was destined to influence contemporary and modern music, and to leave his foot-print in the Sands of Time.

1938·GEORGE ANTHEIL

George Gershwin was one of those rarest of composers, a composer of *ideas!* When George wrote something it was undeniably an idea. It stuck to you whether you liked it or not. You never managed to shake it off again. And, sooner or later, you were bound to like it and even to love it.

Many of this generation of symphonic composers have been sadly remiss in recognizing this quality of one of our greatest American composers. Scarcely a one of them but did not write about George at one time or another, yet their writings always betrayed a faint note of condescension, frankly, a condescension that was as ill-mannered as it was ignorant. Only one of them—Virgil Thomson—ever really recognized the true worth of Gershwin, but he restricted his praise to the sheerly oral; his writings on Gershwin, on the contrary, were often as condescending as the others. And since George's death the situation has remained unchanged. Of course many great conductors, musicians, critics, and even composers, of America have hastened to write fine words about George, but, at least up until now, America's "recognized-aboard" serious symphonic composers have remained strangely silent.

I resented this attitude upon their part, even before George's death. Only a few days before he died, I promised him to make answer to them. It was at a concert George and I were attending together in Hollywood. I assured him then that I would not mince words.

Fellow composers were never fair to George. They never *wanted* to understand him. They wrote patronizing articles about his opera *Porgy and Bess,* and never once attempted to see the magnificent sweep of music behind it; they said, in simple effect, that he was a better Broadway composer, and a worse symphonic one. They pounced upon his crudities, his Debussian cadenzas, his early ignorance of the symphonic forms; never once did they allow him to enter their ranks. Perhaps one cannot entirely blame them; the *American* composer of today is really badly put upon. He is infinitely worse off than the European composer. Nine times out of ten he is miserably poor; George, on the other hand, was rich.

But George, like another composer in another time—Franz Liszt— *supported* a good many poor American composers; even at the time of his death in Hollywood I personally knew of four American white hopes whom George was supporting and this is the first time that this fact has been made known. Throughout the long years *he* never said a word about it to anyone.

Then, too, George was famous. He had written a *Rhapsody in Blue,* a marvelously flamboyant piece full of breath-taking Americana, and this piece was played the width and breadth of the world's continents: *their* pieces, on the other hand, were given one or two performances by one or two of America's great symphony orchestras—and dropped. When Virgil Thomson grew famous (with the performance of his *Four Saints in Three Acts*) he also waxed genial; he found—so he told me—that *"Gershwin is the greatest of American composers."*

Life without tremendous success—especially when one seeks it dearly —is an unhappy proposition. No, we cannot blame American composers whom fortune has not smiled upon, too bitterly.

116

For the American composer, although recognized abroad, is not justly recognized in his own land. Therefore he is usually an embittered person, warped in his judgments of all music except his own, and the milk of human kindness does not flow within his critical writings.

George Gershwin has been recognized by everybody except those whose admiration and understanding he most craved—the American Composer. The admiration of the Coplands, the Sessions, the Thomsons, the Jacobies, and the rest of this special contemporaneous group which undoubtedly contains the very best of America's creative musical talent. I do not know why George craved this, for he certainly never needed their admiration, but he was hurt by their misunderstandings of his work, and their frequent criticisms wounded him.

In the future they will write differently, of course. Bitter or not, they are intelligent men, and it is written upon the wall that Gershwin's occasional crudities, his Debussianisms, his early awkward technique, are already beginning to soften with time, and that it is no longer important whether the middle section of his *Rhapsody in Blue* is or is not pure Post-Impressionism. The *intelligent* musicians of the future cannot certainly be interested in these picayune "flaws"—if truly "flaws" they be—in view of one great and tremendous thing—*George Gershwin wrote music!*

An idiotic statement, perhaps, but nevertheless a singularly timely one. Curiously enough, very few American composers have ever written *music*. Years ago Paul Rosenfeld wrote, and justly, that American composers had ever been prone to bring forth their musical ideas "still-born"; in other words, no matter how often American symphonic compositions were played, their ideas never really gripped into the human ear and held it. For me, at least, this statement would still seem to hold true. I hear innumerable compositions on the American theme, but seldom does any of this music contain a musical idea gripping enough to arrest musical attention. American music is mainly "idealess" music, composed with skill, technique, and taste, but essentially "still-born."

Most of it is not truly "music."

George Gershwin's music was always music. It was flamboyant, angular, often tasteless, and certainly lacked a certain amount of technical skill; but it was music. And it will be music many, many years from now.

That is only because George Gershwin, like Tschaikowsky before him, was a composer of ideas instead of ideals. Tschaikowsky, incidentally, left ideals and aesthetics to "The Russian Five" who loved nothing better than to get into idealistic and nationalistic arguments the whole night through. On the other hand, Tschaikowsky composed a lot of works, but "The Russian Five," outside of possibly Rimsky-Korsakov, composed a comparative few—albeit lovely ones. George was like Tschaikowsky, he loved composing, and he hated talking. His medium was music, and he used his medium.

He learned, for instance, that like literary ideas, musical ideas must always be arresting to hold *mass* attention. Like Beethoven, he *worked* upon his musical ideas. Not just any string of notes became a "theme" to him. He coaxed, wheedled, threatened, and sweated a given string of notes into a "theme," a melody that he himself loved.

And once having learned the most prime fundamental about all music writing—to be able to produce challenging *ideas*, George Gershwin went about the business of learning how to put them into better musical patterns. He was progressing so rapidly that it is now almost certain had he lived he surely would have jumped this last of all hurdles to a truly tremendous musical stature.

The fact that he was cut off in his youth does not prevent him from being one of the greatest American composers of all time. George Gershwin WAS a GREAT composer. He had in abundance the real stuff of which great music is made. He compelled the great masses to recognize it, and he is compelling all of us to recognize it.

And each of us mourns his tragic and too youthful passing.

For whatever his flaws, the flaws of George Gershwin are the flaws of America. He mirrored us, exactly. We need only to look into his music to see a whole period of our history exactly stated.

And upon the walls of countless music libraries existing far into the future there will soon be a shelf labelled "American Music." Upon one part of this shelf—that part labelled 1920 to 1937—one will never miss the name of George Gershwin.

That is immortality, and it is a thing that no whit of our writings here, either for or against, will ever detract; it is a thing that time cannot or will not alter; it is an honor that will be accorded to few other composers of our time; it is a thing that George, perhaps, never really expected.

He merely wanted, and hoped for unimportant and little-needed recognition of his contemporaries.

Composers, let us give that to him. We, all of us today need to remember, as he always knew, that music is music, and it must press close to the heart. So, hats off, to *George Gershwin—American Composer, 1898 - 1937 A. D.*

J E R O M E
1938 · K E R N

There never was anything puny or insignificant about the life, work or opinions of George Gershwin.

He lived, labored, played, exulted and suffered with bigness and gusto. It was some other contemporary, definitely *not* George, who was the subject of Thomas Mann's observation, "Why does he make himself so little? Surely, he is not that big."

There is not much that this unpracticed pen can add to the volumes already written in critical survey of George's work; yet one utterance may be recorded which came from the heart of the man and is illustrative of his stature. It came at the crossroads of his career, long after his dissatisfaction with Broadway musical comedy; even after he had unfolded his pinions and lifted himself into the realm of serious music: "Do you think," he asked with naïveté, "that now I am capable of grand opera? Because, you know," he continued, "all I've got is a lot of talent and plenty of *chutzpah.*"

It was then that these ears realized that they were listening to a man touched with greatness.

120

HAROLD
1937·ARLEN

I am still a part of the world that George Gershwin sprang from and never abandoned. I am very proud of the fact that during the six months just prior to George's death, we became great friends, and in playing with him and talking to him, I came to the complete realization that as a person, he bubbled just as much as his music does. That is why I believe that anyone who knows George's work, knows George. The humor, the satire, the playfulness of most of his melodic phrases were the natural expression of the man.

But it might come as a surprise to many who know the Gershwin legend of the man's excitement over his own work and his enthusiastic appreciation of every contribution he had to make, to learn that he also had a very eager enthusiasm and whole-hearted appreciation for what a great many of us were writing. At odd moments, at most unexpected times, he would be interested enough to tell us something nice about our work. And somehow or other, when George said something nice about my work, I had the grand feeling that he meant what he said and that it was not just a case of saying the right thing. In fact, that was what characterized all of George's comments. There was a constructive insight in what he said which, in my case, helped me form a certain sense of musical values and aided me in becoming more directional.

If, sometimes, we song writers aren't as nice to each other as we might be in judging our respective efforts, if sometimes we look for flaws, instead of relaxing and abandoning ourselves to the mood and spirit of each other's music, let us recall how spontaneously George reacted to many of our songs as they were issued.

I know a certain young composer who was hailed in the lobby of Carnegie Hall one night, when George was the featured artist in the playing of his own composition with a symphony orchestra, with: "Hey, kid, that new song of yours is a pip." This from a man whose mind was supposed to be full of his own importance and the importance of the moment. I can recall an incident when Irving Berlin told a song writer that George had pointed out that this young man's latest effort had demonstrated a particularly original bit of melodic construction in that there was no repetition of phrase from bar to bar in the main theme. This is first-hand information. I was the composer in both cases, and I could go on with many more such instances from the time when I played the piano in the pit orchestra of the *Scandals* up to a few weeks prior to George's passing.

In his own radio programs, George devoted a certain amount of time to introducing some of the younger composers and playing their music, or having them play their own music. And it was not just to encourage these young composers, but to let the radio audience know that he considered them clever writers and liked their work. Dana Suesse, Rube Bloom, Oscar Levant, and various others, he sponsored in this fashion.

Was it that he watched Tin Pan Alley, which had been his breeding ground, to see whether it might not become a breeding ground for others who would make important contributions to American music?

122

LEONARD
1938·LIEBLING

I like to remember that morning in 1924, when Paul Whiteman telephoned to me in New York and asked me to hurry over to the Palais Royal and hear one of his rehearsals at that dance resort. "I think I've got hold of something you might like to sharpen your teeth on," was his cryptic inducement, "and I don't mean the luncheon I'll buy you afterward."

Arrived at the Palais, which quite belied its name at that early hour, I found the orchestra seated on the platform and the sweater-attired maestro in animated consultation with a coatless and vestless young man, both leaning over the piano and discussing a pencilled manuscript on the rack. All about chairs were piled on tables, and kneeling scrubwomen slid about mopping up the debris of the night before.

"Hello, Leonard," yelled Paul, "I want you to listen to this thing. It's by George Gershwin. You know him, don't you? He's done some great stuff for a lot of shows." George and I, unacquainted, shook hands.

Then he and the orchestra played "this thing," and I was frankly uncertain whether I liked it or not. The exotic harmonies and piquant rhythms caught me, and so did the chief broad melody for strings, although it seemed to suggest Tschaikowsky to me at the moment. Paul walked over and asked my opinion just as George joined us.

I answered with the caution of a professional critic: "Well, it's the sort of music one ought to hear at least twice before making up one's

123

mind." "Shall we play it again?" said George to Paul, and they did. The second try fixed me.

"Fine! Splendid!" was my honest reaction; "what do you call it?"

"*Rhapsody in Blue,*" came from George.

Paul, several others and I went to the Tavern for lunch, where the conductor asked us whether we thought him foolish for dreaming that he would like to invade the "classical" precincts by giving a concert in Aeolian Hall. "I have a great following in the popular field, and I'm making a heap of money," he told us; "do you think I'd be risking the loss of both, if you critical undertakers socked me"—looking hard at me—"and sent me back to Broadway with my tail between my legs?" I pointed out that Paul was getting a fortune from the Palais, the Ziegfeld Follies and the Victor Record people, and could afford to tell the critics to go to Helvetia.

"Would any of the big guns in the highbrow musical racket come to the concert?" Paul went on, "and can I send them boxes and say that Leonard Liebling suggested it?"

I made a list on the back of the menu, and said to Paul, "Try to keep them away." Paul sent them boxes. They all came. Then was history made for him and George, and the *Rhapsody in Blue.* Some of those present at Aeolian Hall on February 12, 1924, were Serge Rachmaninoff, Leopold Godowsky, Willem Mengelberg, Josef Stransky, Leopold Stokowski, Victor Herbert, Walter Damrosch, Jascha Heifetz, Mischa Elman, Fritz Kreisler, John Philip Sousa, and other musical Big Berthas.

During ensuing years George and I met frequently and visited at each other's homes. I attended all the premieres of his major works, and witnessed his triumphs on those occasions, including his playing of the *Rhap-*

124

sody with the Minneapolis Orchestra in its home town. Before that engagement, Mr. McKnight, chairman of the board, wired me, "Do you think that is the kind of music we ought to give our public?" I answered: "It is the kind of music your public would resent not being given."

Two other occasions stand out in my memory. When Oscar Strauss came to America to lead the revival of his *Chocolate Soldier,* George gave a midnight party at his place for the visitor following the premiere of his operetta. After supper the host pushed Strauss over to the piano and made him play his music from various scores. At last George said quite earnestly, "I wish you'd teach me how to write Viennese waltzes." "I will," Strauss replied, "if you'll teach me how to write jazz."

While George was busy on the composition of *Porgy and Bess,* he spent a week in Saratoga, where I saw him at the races. "How's the opera coming on?" I inquired.

"Too fast! I've got too many ideas and have to keep on scrapping them."

"What style of music is it?"

"American, of course, in the modern idiom, but just the same, a cross between *Meistersinger* and *Madame Butterfly.* Are those models good enough?" I thought so.

I have set down merely some episodes in the foregoing lines. They are not intended to be an analysis or even an estimate of George Gershwin's musical qualities and methods, to which sufficient homage is paid on other pages of this book. My own summed valuation of the Gershwin abilities is that he voiced authentically the musical spirit of his period in American civilization. I can think of no higher achievement in any artistic endeavor.

125

OTTO H.
1929·KAHN

George Gershwin is a leader of young America in music, in the same sense in which Lindbergh is the leader of young America in aviation. And in more than one respect, he has qualities similar to those of the gallant and attractive Colonel, qualities which we like to consider characteristic of the best type of young America. He has the same unspoilableness,—if I may coin a word,—the same engaging and unassuming ways, the same simple dignity and dislike of show, the same absence of affectation, the same direct, uncomplicated, naïve, "Parsifalesque" outlook upon life and upon his task.

They are a fine lot, take them by and large, these American "kids" of our day, male and female. They are full of talent and of courage. They have a peculiar inner cleanliness and freshness and spontaneousness.

Proceeding without any definite guidance, uncertainly as yet, sometimes mistakenly, but intensely and sincerely, they present the highly interesting phenomenon of a generation groping to find the way for a franker and fuller life than that of its progenitors, trying to ascertain what are genuine values and what are things no longer in tune with our day.

Crude and turbulent sometimes, and a little bit too cocksure, they are serious in purpose, and many of them—more indeed than surface appearance would indicate—are determinedly seeking to aim high.

There is no better raw material to be found anywhere. Below their apparent "hard-boiledness" and sophistication, there is a groping, un-admitted, sometimes uncouth, often unconscious prompting of idealism —a note welcome and needed in the midst of the colossal sweep of the nation's material occupations, and the resulting tendency towards actual, mental and psychic systematization.

And George Gershwin, without self-seeking or self-consciousness, and just because of that, is one of their typical examples, and in his art, thoroughly and uncompromisingly American as it is, one of their fore-most spokesmen. In the rhythm, the melody, the humor, the grace, the rush and sweep and dynamics of his compositions, he expresses the genius of young America.

Now, in that genius of young America, there is one note rather con-spicuous by its absence. It is the note that sounds a legacy of sorrow, a note that springs from the deepest stirrings of the soul of the race. The Ameri-can nation has not known the suffering, the tragedies, the sacrifices, the privations, nor the mellow and deep-rooted romance, which are the age-old inheritance of the peoples of Europe.

The path of America—since she became a nation—has been all too smooth perhaps, too uniformly successful. Mercifully, she has been spared in her development (relatively speaking, at least) the ordeal of deep an-guish, besetting care and heart-searching tribulations, which mark the history of the older nations,—except only the epic tragedy of the Civil War. At that time, the soul of the nation was stirred to its very depth, and out of its profundity it did bring forth the noblest, most moving and most beautiful figure among the public men of all history, Abraham Lincoln.

Now, far be it from me to wish any tragedy to come into the life of this nation for the sake of chastening its soul, or into the life of George

Gershwin, for the sake of deepening his art. But I do want to quote to him a few verses (by Thomas Hardy, I believe) which I came across the other day and which are supposed to relate to America:

> "I shrink to see a modern coast
>   Whose riper times have yet to be;
>   Where the new regions claim them free
>   From that long drip of human tears
>   Which peoples old in tragedy
>   Have left upon the centuried years."

The "long drip of human tears," my dear George! They have great and strange and beautiful power, those human tears. They fertilize the deepest roots of art, and from them flowers spring of a loveliness and perfume that no other moisture can produce.

I believe in you with full faith and admiration, in your personality, in your gifts, in your art, in your future, in your significance in the field of American music, and I wish you well with all my heart. And just because of that I could wish for you an experience—not too prolonged—of that driving storm and stress of the emotions, of that solitary wrestling with your own soul, of that aloofness, for a while, from the actions and distractions of the everyday world, which are the most effective ingredients for the deepening and mellowing and the complete development, energizing and revealment, of an artist's inner being and spiritual powers.

GILBERT
1934·SELDES

It is more than ten years since I heard George Gershwin betray any interest in the opinions of critics, so I hope he will be not too much offended at being considered a case. Like most other human beings, Gershwin has been pushed around a bit, but on the whole he hasn't been pushed out of his own direction. He knows what he is doing, even when he is doing too much or doing the wrong thing. A long time ago he wasn't feeling well and his doctor put him on a régime; and Gershwin had a little notebook in which he recorded his diet and other details; he knew exactly what he was doing. I do not suppose he has a notebook with charts for his musical progress, but he is a young man with assurance. If he is going to do an opera this year, you may be sure that this fits into a general plan which may include a movie theme song or a tone poem or a popular melody for next year. If he decides not to compose for six months and amuse himself by painting he will have in mind the results of his vacation on the next season's output. There is nothing calculating or timid about this; Gershwin will try anything because he is really Kipling's child with his 'satiable curiosity. At the same time he is too well established to be blown away by any wind of chance.

I don't know any popular American composer who is brighter, more generally aware, more likely to give you a mental satisfaction than Gershwin, and, the moment this is said, I ought to go on and indicate my doubt whether Gershwin is really a popular composer at all. I know all about the *Rhapsody in Blue,* having been present (if I may make so bold) at its conception; I also walked into the Palais Royal when it was merely a rehearsal hall and heard the first complete run-through with Paul Whiteman's orchestra; and lived one summer next to anonymous neighbors who owned (I suppose) only one record and played it all the time, the same *Rhapsody,* which still, to my mind, has an admirable slow movement and is a delightful piece. Or four or five delightful pieces loosely strung together. But the *Rhapsody* alone doesn't make Gershwin a popular composer—as he was when he wrote *Swanee. Swanee* was just Gershwin writing a Mammy song for Al Jolson, but it was one of the best and it is the sort of thing Gershwin wouldn't be found dead with today. He could write it and write rings around it and kid Mammy's kerchief off it, but he wouldn't sincerely write a simple although synthetic song like *Swanee* again. He has learned better and has become our foremost composer of satirical operettas.

The thing to remember in this connection is that his famous forerunner, Sir Arthur Sullivan, never forgot how to write sentimental lyrics and had a strain of religiosity in him which came out in *The Lost Chord.*

There is a famous bit of dialogue along Tin Pan Alley: How long will Gershwin's music live? As long as Gershwin is alive to play it! He loves a piano, and it is said that no amount of sarcasm and no show of force will keep him away—and he is right, because he is one of the most entertaining of all pianists. When Eva Gauthier put a group of his songs on a recital program, Gershwin played the accompaniments and sent an audience into hysterics of delight by throwing in a few bars of Scheherezade as backing for his own *Stairway to Paradise* and getting back to business before anyone knew what had happened. His darting mind controls his darting

130

fingers, his playing is as amusing as his melodies are tricky and smart. But he pays for this skill.

Popular music used to be written to be sung; then to be danced to; and now it is written to be played. Irving Berlin not only has gone through all three stages, but goes through them year after year, which accounts for his preëminent position as a popular composer—in *As Thousands Cheer* you have the *Easter Parade* to sing; the *Rice in China* song to dance to; and *Heat Wave,* a rhythm song, to listen to. Jerome Kern's great songs, and they include the best of our time, are all songs to be sung. And Gershwin's become more and more songs to be played. They are masterly; *I've Got Rhythm* (and *could* you ask for anything more?), *Strike Up The Band, Sam and Delilah,* and the best thing in two successive shows, *Wintergreen for President.* But who can forget it?

Not Gershwin, in any case. What he can play on the piano—and he can play anything—he puts down on paper, forgetting that we who listen are not gifted with his mastery of complicated rhythms. So he composes to be heard, not to be sung. He is lucky because we are becoming a nation of listeners, thanks to the radio. But he is losing ground as a pure troubadour. He has stopped singing himself.

Privately there is a lot of simplicity in Gershwin. He is young, he is successful, he enjoys his success. Whenever you see him, he is overwhelmed in work, mad about some new dancer or singer who is going to put over something he has composed, rehearsing with a cigar handy, dashing back to his penthouse which was modern (and strikingly and comfortably modern) at the very beginning of the rage for modern, thinking about going to Hollywood, discussing a new lyric with his brother Ira who lives on the same terrace and comes in ready with something intricate in rhyme-schemes to make sure that brother George doesn't fall back on June and moon. He is tall and dark and looks well in tails and always looks a little self-conscious when he is not working; not uncomfortable in the world of expensive clubs, but aware of them; not overcome by people nearly as famous as himself, but nodding to them; not dazzled but pleased.

That likeable simplicity doesn't come out in his work which gets more complicated and interesting and brittle and unmelodious with every year. It is as if Gershwin were writing for the five thousand people who go to the Lido, know the one best club in London, can't count above 21 in New York, and depend on Elsa Maxwell for a good time. Those five thousand —perhaps there are a few more—making up the bulk of the first week's audiences at a new show, can give a musical piece an invisible banner to fly from the theatre's marquee, worth as much as a Pulitzer prize; the wit and intelligence which please them can then bring in the fifty thousand more who are needed to pay off the cost of production. But they cannot make a popular composer.

At bottom, I do not believe that Gershwin is a satirist. I can't be sure, but I do not think he has suffered enough or thought enough; he hasn't had time, success coming to him early, frequently and abundantly. I think he has been carried away by the satire of others. There was a middle point when Gershwin wrote a musical burlesque with lyrics by Brian Hooker, of which the masterpiece, words and music, was *Innocent Ingenue* (Baby). The show was not a success and the songs are remembered by perhaps a dozen people, of whom I am the most persistent. Here you had a sweet melody with a touch of mockery on the word "Baby"; but when you come to *Of Thee I Sing, Baby*, the satire is everything. It rises to a high level of satisfaction when you dance off with a hey-nonny-nonny and a hotchacha or hear cheers for your own country and s-s-s for the Swiss, the music in these cases being apt and full of bright little ideas. There isn't anyone else who could let music ripple so freely around the Supreme Court and the Senate and Communists and depressions. A touch of parody here, a shift of emphasis or rhythm making a marching song pompous and ridiculous, a sharp or a flat when you are not expecting either to show that a love song isn't to be taken seriously, and a lightness of touch everywhere, making the whole gay and bright—Gershwin has them in profusion, he is a cascade of little inventions, he gives you good times.

The reason is that he has a good time himself with his music. When he discovered himself on the road to a new position in America—a composer of jazz who was to be played by symphony orchestras—he began to study orchestration, fascinated by it, by the instruments and their voices. He was young enough not to abandon the effort to learn all the technical business of writing music: harmony and counterpoint and dividing voices. And he didn't let his concert work slide, either; from a trip abroad he brought back *An American in Paris* and he wrote a concerto for orchestra and himself ("for orchestra and piano" on the programs, of course, and I believe others have played it, but probably not so well). In the old days when Otto H. Kahn was being liberally misquoted as wanting a "jazz opera" for the Metropolitan, Gershwin was coming over the horizon as the man who might make what Kahn really wanted, a grand opera using the rhythms of American popular music. My own guess is that Gershwin will do better with an American ballet.

Wealth, society, intellectuals—all the things which distract a composer of popular song—seem to have no bad effect on ballet. Diaghileff was a frequenter of the Lido and his first nights in Paris were all society and arts and letters, and his ballets were great. And Gershwin is writing intricate music to which American dance steps fit. Let an idea hover in the air, let the right people present it to him appealingly, and he will compose a ballet which may not have the emotion of Strawinsky—why the devil should it?—but, I'll take a bet, will be as entertaining as anything the sacred Six of Paris ever made.

I'd rather see him do that than do an operatic version of *Porgy* which I never succumbed to in the first place. I'd rather see him doing a ballet than have him write songs which might have been written by Cole Porter (only Gershwin's are essentially innocent). Give a good ballet master the *Stairway to Paradise* (reworked by the author, because it is over ten years old now and Gershwin has learned a lot) and you'd have the foundation of a ballet right there. Or, his own variations on *I've Got Rhythm*. Or anything he has written in five years.

It is intelligent of me to look to the future instead of the past. I don't believe that the spring of melody in Gershwin has dried up; you catch a few bars now and then which are a pure pleasure. Something might happen and he might do something lyrical, something to shout under the shower. But I am not going to shed tears if he doesn't; I am not even going to say that he is a spoiled composer of popular songs. He has gone on to something else. He has only to keep going until he has pushed through the things and people which now divert or distract him. If he is to be a satirist, he has eventually to find the things he himself is satirical about—I should think he would find plenty. When he does, he will be saying something instead of saying something about something else. That is his present position—one step removed from his own expression, taking things a little at second hand and making them first rate by his prodigious talent. And it is so prodigious that he can afford to be spendthrift with it. And is.

134

RUDY
1938·VALLEE

I knew George Gershwin only slightly and I could hardly claim being an intimate friend of his although I do feel I was numbered among his friendly acquaintances.

Of course, when a student at Yale, playing with dance orchestras in order to pay my way through school, I became acquainted with George through his excellent compositions, especially the songs from the *Scandals* and the brilliant shows he wrote during the years of 1923 through 1927. In fact, the more we played his compositions, the more I enjoyed playing them. They offered a means of really pouring forth some of my emotions which I felt upon playing the compositions. Therefore, I was tremendously flattered when, in 1929 at a society party, Mr. Gershwin and I both appeared gratis as supporters of a very worthy charity cause. The warmth displayed by this élite audience towards him was tremendous. He played just a few simple tunes for them.

The closest association I had with him was in Washington when we both fought for the American Society of Composers, Authors, and Publishers and the fine ideals in protecting its membership and fighting for proper remuneration for its creators. Both of us testified in Washington before the Senate Committee. There, I had several chats with him and became indeed friendly.

On one of our broadcasts, he played one of his concertos. It was difficult to conduct but after working on it, I won the commendation of the artist. I found him to be intelligent, shy, reticent, clean-cut, honest and an extremely likeable genius. I use the word genius very sparingly and I felt Gershwin was truly a great musician.

1938·HENRY A. BOTKIN

A number of years ago George Gershwin experienced his first thrill from a contemporary painting and promptly purchased it with great enthusiasm. At that time he never considered himself a great collector or a champion of modern painting. He bought the canvas because he liked it and wanted it about. It was this irresistible impulse that led to further purchases and the beginning of a most significant collection. Our frequent visits to the galleries and studios of various artists here and abroad displayed George's intense feeling and joy in pictures and painting. The spirit of his music and its relation to art became more and more evident. He realized that his rhythms and their rhythms had many common factors.

His collection has evolved logically and always displays a singleness of purpose and inspiration. He never pretended to possess a scholarly group of paintings, there were no "old" pictures and he never posed as an art historian or expert. He has striven for examples that seemed to be the most vital and the most stimulating. The careful subtle patterning, the rich color, together with the sombre power and fine sentiment found in the various canvases have produced a deep, spontaneous artistic excitement for the collector. During our many years of close relationship, I have noted how the special quality of his extraordinary music has given proof of the similarity of imaginative tendencies and strong spiritual kinship to these many striking achievements in paint. His painting and collecting

137

have resulted in the assimilation of aesthetic nourishment for his musical genius. He was always interested in the various movements of art, but never allowed himself to follow the dictates of fashion. His pictures were not considered as ornaments or decorations for his walls and he was not affected by any intellectual snobbishness.

Art to George seemed ever aglow with passionate life and proved his love for the world of today. Whether he was composing, searching for new masterpieces, painting or joining in a festive evening, he brought to the occasion all the vigor and vital force that was in him. In his adventures in art, if at times he seemed impulsive and spontaneous, he was also simple and highly intelligent. Thus it was that nine years sufficed to bring together one of the most significant collections of modern art in America as well as a group of his own paintings. The collection consists of over a hundred examples of paintings and sculpture, drawings, prints, etc., and though it has no pretence to completeness, it contains some of the greatest examples of contemporary painting that can be found in this country.

George never collected a list of names and it was only the quality of the individual canvases that counted. Some of the most interesting works are the products of the unknown younger painters and not of the men whose names are so familiar to us. They have a definite place in his collection and George championed and assisted them at all times.

Besides paintings in oil by the masters, he had gathered a most varied group of important examples of Negro sculpture, together with drawings, rare water colors and lithographs. He never confined himself to the paintings of any one group or country, but was always interested in the various movements and schools of art. He possessed some of the most important examples of contemporary art by the dominating personalities in the

138

American art world. Though he was not always sympathetic to abstract art, he studied and collected Kandinsky, Leger, Masson and others. He was extremely interested in Picasso, Utrillo, De Segonzac, Derain and Rousseau. He also possessed some of the outstanding examples of the American school, as, Eilshemius, Bellows, Sterne, Weber and Benton. In recent years his collection had outgrown several large apartments and overflowed into the homes of his friends and family, but he carried on to the last as one of the most intrepid of the younger collectors of today.

George himself began painting in 1929 and after some encouragement and assistance on my part revealed a profound and genuine talent. As his painting progressed, he displayed how the specific moods of his musical compositions had given a vital form and emotional strength to his paintings. The intense, dynamic impulses of his music became the dominating force in his painting. He was a good student and as his talent began to assert itself he spent more and more time in the art galleries and museums. He permitted himself to become soaked in the culture of painting and made many visits to the various galleries and the studios of painters so that he could acquaint himself more fully with the different principles and techniques. The work of Rouault was especially close to him and he was constantly enthralled by the life and spirit that animated his work. He wanted his own pictures and music to possess the same breathtaking power and depth. He strove constantly to master the same bold combination of accessories that he possessed as a composer. In his various paintings and especially his portraits he tried for the precise contour that defined the form and constantly concerned himself with composition and color.

His paintings called for no special aesthetic theories or psychology.

In his many drawings of various degrees of completion—and there are over a hundred—he demonstrated an amazing skill as a draughtsman. His constant application and the quantity of the works left behind him are a sufficient indication of his love and desire to contribute something truly important. As I observed his progress, I noticed especially how he tried to supply to his painting the same warmth, enthusiasm and power that characterized his music.

He was especially interested in people and portraiture and he had a decided talent for presenting a whole personality in a small sketch. This is shown in the studies of Adolph Lewisohn, Maurice Sterne and others. These studies, which were achieved in a few minutes, were later used as material for his paintings in oil. In his self-portrait, "Checked Sweater," he built up his forms with layer upon layer of pigment and the result is a highly dramatic painting of emotional effectiveness, rich and alive. In the portrait of "Schoenberg" he has solved an extremely interesting plastic problem and achieved a dynamic, expressive painting. This canvas is not only intense and vivid but shows a distinct admiration and respect for his sitter. As a man richly gifted in both head and heart, he constantly tried to endow his models with a most sensitive rendering of their individual character.

Besides being an able draughtsman, he possessed a compelling and powerful line and was able to achieve results with the most economical of means. One has only to observe the exquisite drawings of "Girl Reading," his brother "Ira" and "Henry Botkin," which could have been the work of Picasso or Dufy.

He always made me believe that painting was a little in advance of music in expressing ideas and moods. If he was interested in the modern trends in art it was because they had the same qualities as the music with which he was concerned. He once told me when we were discussing the French painter Rouault, "I am keen for dissonance; the obvious bores me. The new music and the new art are similar in rhythm, they share a sombre power and fine sentiment."

George had an instinctive sense of art's creative processes and was especially sensitive to rhythm. In quiet and reticent tones he has painted some still lifes and landscapes and though they did not come as easily as the portraits, they show a richness and solidity, together with a considerable amount of assurance. He worked in water color and in the study of "My Studio—Folly Beach," I am struck by the extraordinary feeling of graphic and pictorial beauty. It seems to have been rendered with a childish, primitive violence and yet possesses an opulence of beauty.

In the painting of "My Grandfather," his style was somewhat like folk art. Some of his paintings possess deep, sonorous tones, as the picture of "Jerome Kern," which represents one of the highest summits of his achievements. The head seems to emerge from a cavern of shadows, each tone resounds like a note of music. Rhythm by Gershwin in music would have a definite place in his painting. He was trying to achieve a kind of "melodic" painting, the sort which creates a harmonious relation between man and the world around him.

His work was never self-consciously modern and he always avoided distracting mannerisms and surface cleverness. In all his later work he had developed a mastery of his craft and even though he found time to create only small studies, they were never mere exercises but self-contained examples of art.

His brother Ira became enthusiastic about painting at the same time and joined him in the new pursuit. It was common for friends to drop around to their penthouse and find each at his easel busily laying on color when they should have been completing a new score. George was so encouraged by the praise of many eminent artists that there were periods when his paints and brushes almost weaned him away from his music. When we lived on Folly Island near Charleston and George was busily engaged in writing *Porgy and Bess,* he would abandon his piano often to rush out and join me in painting the picturesque Negro shacks. He painted and made sketches during his travels and his sketch box and easel were always part of his baggage.

Any judgment on the art of George Gershwin at this time can represent little more than a personal opinion. There is no doubt that he would have won increasing recognition had he lived, and if he was not famous as a painter it was merely because his activities as a composer had not given him sufficient opportunity to paint. His work was at all times serious and not a composer's pastime and every effort showed an earnestness and sincere love. I am confident with time his talent might have flowered into something comparable to his genius as a composer. As Mr. Frank Crowninshield says in his introduction to the catalogue of the Gershwin Exhibition, "George had a way of regarding his painting and his music as almost interchangeable phenomena. They sprang, he felt, from the same Freudian elements in him, one emerging as sight, the other as sound. The first he shaped with a brush, the second with a goose-quill."

To the world at large George Gershwin will always be known as one of the foremost exponents of modern American music. He also will be remembered as a man who possessed an almost feverish and unquenchable enthusiasm for the fine arts. It was evident on observing his posthumous one-man show which was held at the Marie Harriman Gallery in New York City, in December, 1937, that he aspired to equal his achievements as a composer. He was on his way to that goal and from tactile apperception he was able to move steadily toward a truly optical vision that would have enabled him to create a personal style in keeping with his temperament. The task that he was unable to bring to fruition bears the indelible imprint of his genius and personality. In the words of Henry McBride, the noted art critic, "if the soul be great, all expressions emanating from that soul must be great."

"I AM
A MODERN
ROMANTIC"
GEORGE
GERSHWIN

ORCHID, 1934

MY GRANDFATHER, 1933

MOTHER, 1933

FATHER, 1933

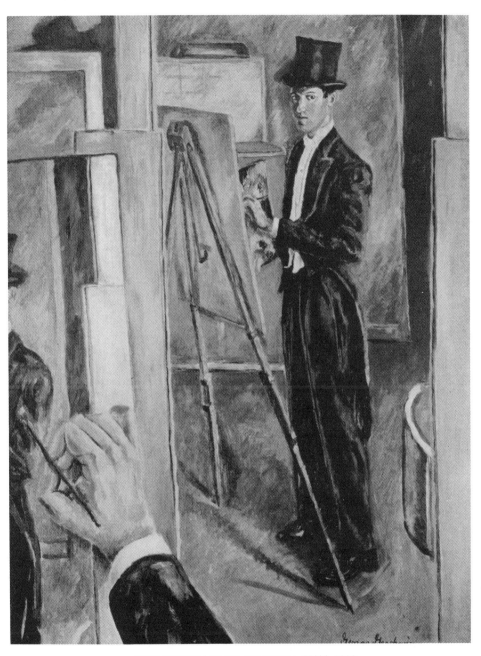

SELF PORTRAIT IN AN OPERA HAT, 1932

HENRY BOTKIN, 1932

GIRL'S HEAD, 1933

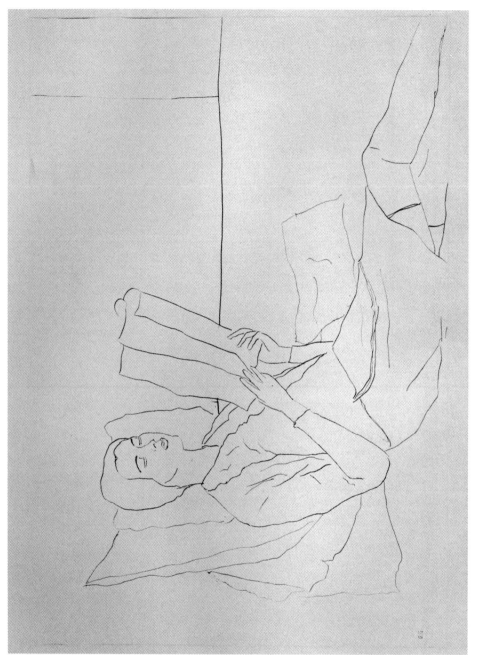

GIRL READING, 1931

NEGRO CHILD, 1933

DUBOSE HEYWARD, 1934

EMILY, 1936

JEROME KERN, 1937

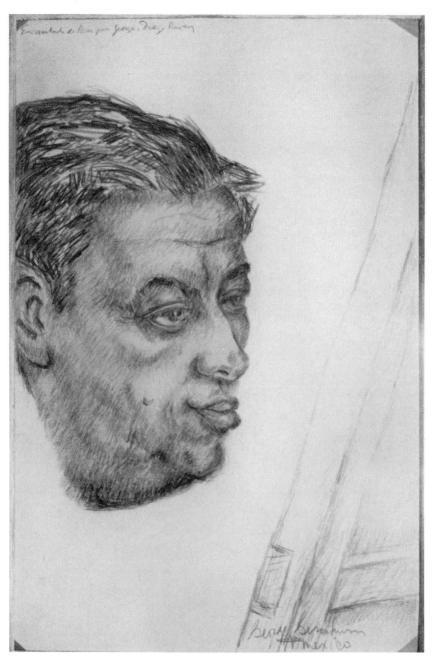

DIEGO RIVERA, 1936

SELF PORTRAIT IN CHECKERED SWEATER, 1936

ARNOLD SCHOENBERG, 1937

NEGRO SCULPTURE, 1934

1938·ISAAC GOLDBERG

Of George Gershwin's music, considered from the technical and the historical aspect, I have said most of what I had to say in my book upon the man and his writings. There is little that I would add, fundamentally, to that account. Moreover, the book is to be expanded and brought up to date in a definitive revision; Ira Gershwin and I shall soon be working upon it. Today I should prefer to write about George the person, as I knew him from our many meetings—kaleidoscopic meetings, I almost said—over many years.

It was through James P. McEvoy that I was finally introduced to him, after a sporadic correspondence. The musical comedy *Show Girl* was playing in Boston, and so were the Symphony "Pops." At that time (1929) the Italian composer, Alfredo Casella, was conducting; he had always been deeply interested in the newer American music, jazz included. *Show Girl,* it happened, contained a ballet founded upon *An American in Paris,* and the piece itself, as originally written, was included upon Casella's program. Which combination of circumstances had resulted, among other things, in bringing McEvoy, Gershwin and me to that particular "Pops" concert.

I had been writing here and there about Gershwin's versatile employment of "blue" notes in his music. Manifestly, a crowded greenroom on a warm summer evening was hardly the place to continue on that note. I have always been averse to meeting people, however famous, on the wing; that evening, too, I demurred. When I had properly shaken hands with the smiling, radiant young composer, his face glistening with unaffected pleasure in his success, I left without a suspicion that we should ever meet again.

A plan was shortly afoot to have the composer's biography written. Not one of your self-conscious, stiff-backed museum accounts, but a lively story befitting the career and the times of a youth still fresh with ideas and hopes for his native music. If I am not mistaken, the notion had first occurred to the New York literary agent, Miss Grace Morse. A number of writers had been suggested to George, but he desired someone with a knowledge of music as well as of writing. In this, I believe (and entirely apart from my later connection with the idea) he was, as in so many other things, intuitively right. I have been offended—and I believe that George was, more than once—by the manner in which persons obviously ignorant of music have written about not only George the personality but George the composer.

Anyway, when I expressed an interest in doing the biography, George remembered, much to my amazement, our meeting in the greenroom of Boston's Symphony Hall; also, he had read my *Story of Gilbert and Sullivan*. And, eventually, because my book on the heavenly twins of English operetta had been published by Simon and Schuster, my book on George was brought out by the same firm. Dick Simon is the musical executant of the combination.

I recall an evening at my home, some years later, in which George, and Hugh Foss (then musical director of the Oxford Press publications), Barry Cerf, Jesus María Sanromá, and Gershwin figured. It was on this evening that Gershwin was introduced by me to the brilliant Sanromá, who was afterwards to become one of the foremost pianistic exponents of Gershwin that we have.

I had arranged with Sanromá, who has an irrepressible sense of humor and card-tricks, to start playing the *Rhapsody in Blue* at a signal. Gershwin was occupied in an adjoining room with Barry Cerf and Hugh Foss, who was dropping cigarette-ash on book-shelves, into the piano strings, into stray hats, and where not else. All at once the strains of the *Rhapsody* arose, and with them, George's ears. He walked straight over to the piano and then and there, I believe, a little history was made. Sanromá and the *Rhapsody* have become closely identified ever since; next to George playing that piece, I have always preferred the gifted Porto-Rican. Sanromá has a remarkable sense of style, and an intuitive affinity to jazz. I wonder that his playing of the *Concerto in F* still remains unrecorded.

I am not (whether you take the expression socially or politically) a party-man. For that reason, I rarely attended the parties that Gershwin gave in his various New York homes. It was a joke between us that I had a standing invitation not to come to any party that he gave. I preferred the more intimate moments, when I might listen to his aims, his wonders, his doubts. From the first I had felt that he was not the man to pursue an intensive course in academic music, so as to make up for what he had missed in his boyhood. Not that I scorn technical knowledge; far from it. George, however, was by nature non-academic, and I have a fear that many a moment of his was spoiled by an excessive consciousness of his academic shortcomings. I was pleased to hear, only the other day, that when George, in Paris, had taken steps toward studying with Ravel, both Nadia Boulanger and Ravel had advised against it, on much the same grounds that I had. Of technically skilled composers we had, and have, a plenty. There has been only one George Gershwin.

I would not have these words understood as implying that—as some commentators have expressed it—George made a mistake in looking toward symphonic and operatic music. Not at all. George's orchestral pieces reveal precisely those defects in structure that one would expect of an intuitive, lyrical, ingenuous nature such as his. His opera, *Porgy and Bess,* likewise, reveals similar defects of structure, of orchestration. Yet his natural gifts easily compensated for these shortcomings, and gave us something that no amount of musical learning could have supplied. This may be one of the definitions of genius. For in George's music there is a vitality that overcomes all else.

I have promised not to discuss, technically, the music of George Gershwin. Some aspects of that music, however, are so clearly the man himself, that to speak of the man, as I wish to do, is inevitably to speak of the music.

That man was, as that music is, honest, real, forthright, unaffected, basically sound. The music, like the man, was forever reaching forward. George had an intense desire to write a few bars that would live. The question, "Do you think anything of mine will live?" was often on his lips, at least when he spoke with me. He had a passionate sense of the people—not an eagerness to compromise with popular taste, or to write down, but to reach that something in them which is the core of universality. Again this was evidence of his lyric, intuitive nature.

His humor, his gaiety, were more in his music (from what I could observe) than in his living. It is symptomatic that while one person will

164

regard George as the American Chopin, another sees in him the American Offenbach. When he wrote *Porgy and Bess* he effected, better than Sullivan or Herbert did, the transition from light opera to opera of more serious cast. There is every reason to believe that had he lived he would have gone on to unmistakable triumphs. For his advance was not a question of more knowledge, but of deepening emotions.

Something in him, even on the threshold of forty, remained eternally boyish. There was a look in his eyes that was the counterpart of his frequent doubts. If it seems strange to say it, I can only offer in support a deep conviction: George had not yet really found himself at the time he died. It was this quality in him, as in his music, that made his music at times so exciting.

I recall once, during the rehearsals of *Strike Up the Band* (the second version, produced in Boston by Edgar Selwyn), that I was taking moving-pictures of him in the Public Gardens. He noticed a heap of dirt by a flower bed. Seizing a twig, he stood before the dirt heap and posed in caricature fashion, as I cranked the camera. "And what's that idea?" I asked. "Call it Gershwin conducting some of his rubbish," he said. This was simply an extreme statement of the way he sometimes felt about his musical gropings. George, of course, never regarded his least work as "rubbish." It was too much a part of himself. Sometimes he ran it down in the hope of being contradicted. I doubt that he was ever deceived by the back-slappers. I never knew a composer who received comment and criticism more eagerly, more gratefully, sometimes, indeed, too humbly.

He was always ready to surrender any part of his score to the requirements of a smooth production. And as for his forbearance with singers who all but assassinated his tunes and Ira's words, it was simply early

Christian, and all but rushed forth to martyrdom. He was so much of the showman that I frequently marveled at his absence of authorial testiness. I wonder whether he enjoyed his commercial experience in Hollywood. I wonder whether he didn't miss the excitement of rehearsals and first-nights—the humanness of the physical theatre, the fluctuating qualities of successive performances, the personal contact with his own work. I know that, at the time of his death, he was looking forward to doing more stage shows, and I could well believe that the stage was his first love and his last.

I find that, his music apart, it is for quiet, unpublic moments that I most remember him: for midnight chats with him and the late Bill Daly (a musician to the finger-tips) in that pleasant penthouse on Riverside Drive; for rehearsals of his unfamiliar *Second Rhapsody,* in its piano version, with the demonic Oscar Levant at the piano with George; for coming in upon him and Madge Kennedy going over *The Man I Love,* which she was to sing at some benefit or other; for nights in vacant theatre auditoriums, while *Strike Up the Band, Of Thee I Sing,* and *Let 'Em Eat Cake* were being prepared for the public. It was at the rehearsals of the first of these that I met, through George and Ira, Messrs. George S. Kaufman and Morrie Ryskind. It is Kaufman, Ryskind, Moss Hart, and the Gershwin brothers, who have given to our country the closest approach we have had to Gilbert and Sullivan and Jacques Offenbach. George was, and the rest of these men are, historical in their lifetime.

The last time I saw George was at the rehearsals and performances of *Porgy and Bess* when it opened in Boston. I can still see tears in the eyes of more than one spectator at the rehearsal, during the scene of the wake. I can recall the aggressive enthusiasm of Sam N. Behrman, the quiet ardor of Ira, the apprehensive satisfaction of DuBose Heyward. I can hear the piercing elegy, *My Man's Gone Now.* How soon it was to begin ringing suddenly in my ears on a sad Sunday, up in Maine, when I was informed over the telephone, late at night, that George had died! Grief has its irrelevancies. As suddenly, I saw myself at lunch with George in Boston's Ritz-Carlton, each of us picking through the menu with hypochondriac appetites. Robert Darrell, at present music critic for *The New Masses,* wrote up that lunch in humorous fashion for a magazine that specialized in phonographic music. Why this scene should come floating through my pain at that moment as the visual accompaniment of George's elegy, I cannot tell. I surrender it to the psycho-analysts, reserving all rights to veto the interpretation.

I remember him for his unaffected friendship, for the undiminishing pleasure of his music, for the simplicity and forthrightness of his character. And now that the first pangs of the loss have subsided, I remember him most of all for his joyous preoccupation with whatever he had in hand. His death was a tragedy—"the greatest I have ever known," as George S. Kaufman wrote to me. The impress of his life, however, was one of vigor, of joy, and it is by his life, not his death, that we shall all wish to remember him.

1938·SAM H. HARRIS

I shall always think of George Gershwin as one of the most valiant persons I have ever known. I never met anyone who seemed to enjoy life to the hilt as he did, or who gloried more in achievement. It was the game more than the reward that delighted him.

A few years ago we used to play golf together at Palm Beach. I can see him now on the links, a gay, tremendously alive, vital figure, bubbling over with zest and enthusiasm. I remember we used to play matches for a stake. I will have to admit that he was a little better than I and told him that I thought he should give me a handicap of at least two strokes, which he did. The first day he won, and when I offered to pay he waved me away and said:

"We'll double on tomorrow's game, Sam."

When tomorrow came, I asked him to give me a handicap of four strokes, and he said okay. He won and again refused to accept my check. The next time we played he said:

"Sam, name your own handicap."

I asked for six strokes and he said, "O.K." He won again. The amount had reached a very substantial figure and I insisted that he would have to let me make good. He jumped into his car and said:

"Forget it, Sam."

"I won't forget it, George," I replied. "You will just have to take my check. A bet's a bet."

"The next time we play I am going to give you a stroke a hole," he shouted as he started the car. "I don't think I can beat you, but that's the only chance you have of winning."

And he was off with a wave of the hand and a chuckle at my discomfiture before I could make any reply. He never would let me pay that bet. The incident was, I think, typical of his attitude towards life. I shall miss him as long as I live. He was not only a friend, but an exhilarating tonic to those who knew him well.

1938·LESTER DONAHUE

So much has been written, with so much more to follow, about George Gershwin and the importance of his pivotal position in the music world, that I hope to confine this brief memoir to some of our meetings in a non-professional world during a friendship which lasted fifteen years.

Musical New York in the winter of 1922-23 was not so Gershwin-conscious as it was to become within a year. Eva Gauthier had not rocked the foundations of Aeolian Hall by singing *I'll Build a Stairway to Paradise* and *Swanee* on her annual program of advanced modern composers, and the *Rhapsody in Blue* was still unwritten.

There were several hostesses in New York at that time who pioneered in mingling musical and theatrical artists with other guests of a more sated social world, and one of the most popular and enterprising of these was Miss Mary Hoyt Wiborg. Her flair for discovering and pursuing obscure genius and future celebrity was well-known, so when she invited me to dine, with Ruth Draper and the Paul Kochanskis, and cross the river to New Jersey to hear the tryout of a new musical comedy I anticipated some sort of pleasant surprise, despite the awkwardness of the evening's schedule and a thorough lack of acquaintance with New Jersey. We listened in a rather dingy theatre to Constance Binney in *The Perfect Lady,* which antithetically became *Sweet Little Devil* before reaching New York, and were captivated by a new quality of joyous rhythm in the score, especially in the song *Virginia,* and went back-stage to meet a very friendly young man named George Gershwin, whose personality seemed as joyous and rhythmic as his music.

"Hoytie" carried him off for supper at her home in lower Fifth Avenue, where many embryonic celebrities were heard before the world knew much about them, and my chief recollection of him that evening is at the piano, playing and singing *Virginia* over and over, with that delightful zest and relish with which he performed his own music, and with the already inevitable black cigar. There was a naïve honesty of enjoyment about him at the piano, which never forsook him. His attitude never approached conceit, and precluded that undercurrent of critical rivalry which usually exists when two or more pianistic prima donnas find themselves at the same party. He swept the atmosphere clean of pedantic rigamarole and delighted the most sedate concert pianists as well as dilettantes with his infectious playing. Perhaps the fact that his superb facility at the piano was merely one of many facets of his talent contributed to the whole-hearted pleasure which he gave his listeners as well as himself.

George became a fixture at "Hoytie's" cosmopolitan and stimulating parties from that night on and also at her sister's, the late Mrs. Sidney Fish, and soon Fifth and Park Avenues were as Gershwin-conscious as Broadway already had become. There were some remarkable evenings of music that winter, with Cole Porter, Artur Rubinstein, Eva Gauthier and others contributing until early hours of the morning after more static dinner guests had departed, and George was invariably generous. No one ever had to urge him to play and to the best of my knowledge no one ever wanted him to stop. He was tremendously acquisitive about all phases of music and impressed me by delving into Bach at a time when he was still regarded only as a brilliant and promising composer of Broadway shows.

Within the year 1924 *George Gershwin* became a household name. The critics as well as the public raved about the *Rhapsody heard 'round the world,* the late Harry Osgood declaring it "a more important contribution to music than Strawinsky's *Le Sacre du Printemps,*" but George remained as serene and unspoiled as before this exciting peak in his career. He began to plan and work on his first concerto, commissioned to be performed by him with Damrosch and the New York Symphony.

It was the *Miracle* year in New York, with continual entertaining for Lady Diana Manners and those other English visitors who have since become more or less permanent, Beatrice Lillie, Gertrude Lawrence, and Noel Coward. George's *Rhapsody* became the theme-song for all these occasions and I remember Christmas Day at Mrs. Fish's on Long Island when thousands of dollars worth of talent performed after luncheon in extraordinary combinations which the public would have paid any price to hear.

Early in 1925 the great Strawinsky conducted a concert of his own compositions and "Hoytie" gave a large party for him afterwards at a friend's home, nearer Carnegie Hall than her own. She assumed that the piano was an adequate, normally-behaved instrument and was obsessed by the idea of having Gershwin and Strawinsky improvise together. After much persuasion the two unwilling victims, strangers until that evening, were seated at the piano, with a brilliant assemblage of all the leading musicians, Fred and Adele Astaire, and several Mrs. Vanderbilts waiting to hear an inspired moment in musical history. Chaliapin stood benevolently in the curve of the piano, his arms raised to conduct. The two great masters of rhythm studied each other for a moment like prize

172

fighters in the ring and then began to play vigorously. Not a sound escaped from the exasperating keyboard. It was a curious contraption connected with a pipe organ in the same room and John Hays Hammond Jr. had discovered that he could lock the piano connection and save both of them from probable embarrassment, an important link in his later friendship with Gershwin and Strawinsky.

From the confusion of memories of those hectic years I recall a delightful party given in George's honor by Dr. and Mrs. Walter Damrosch, following the first performance of his *Concerto in F*. He was very happy that night, pleased with the reception of his concerto and also over his first appearance as pianist with Damrosch at Carnegie Hall. The heated controversy started that evening as to whether George should abandon Broadway and the brilliant musical shows he had given it or continue with concertos, a symphony or two, and an opera for the Metropolitan. He remained less upset by it than some of his friends and steered a clear course through as difficult a path as any composer has had to follow, keeping musical integrity with both sides, as *Porgy and Bess* shows.

Another evening stands out clearly—a distinguished dinner for twelve men which Schuyler Parsons gave in honor of Colonel Lindbergh before his first flight to Mexico. It was *Funny Face* year and I remember the Colonel's keen enjoyment of *S'Wonderful,* which he asked George to repeat; also that my Debussy, wedged between George Gershwin and Cole Porter playing their latest song hits, seemed decidedly on the pallid side. I sat next to George at dinner and he told me about his plans for *An American in Paris,* which he was going to orchestrate himself. He didn't seem to feel the necessity of choosing between two antagonistic musical paths as he accepted both; contributing invaluably to both.

A few months later we continued this conversation in Vienna, where I was playing the Hammond piano on tour. Krenek's *Johnny Spielt Auf* was the sensation of central European opera houses that year and Hammond and I went to hear it the night we reached Vienna. It purported to be American jazz, in conventional operatic setting, composed by a German and sung by a Viennese. Aside from the remarkable scenic and ballet resources of the famous Vienna Opera House it was completely "phoney" and I remarked rather loudly in the foyer that if such an opera were to be done effectively it should be by George Gershwin. Someone behind me said "Oh Yeah" and I turned to find George, Ira and Leonore Gershwin beaming at me. They had come to Paris so that George could write his *American in Paris* to the blare of Montmarte taxi horns and had found far too many insistent friends anxious to entertain them, so had fled to Vienna where they hoped they would know no one.

We all had supper at the Bristol Hotel and enjoyed the following week together. George was very fair about *Johnny Spielt Auf* and contended that it was a worthy effort, but I was quietly pleased the following winter when it was produced at the Metropolitan and several of the critics claimed they had never sufficiently appreciated Gershwin.

George worked all day on *An American in Paris* in Vienna, to loud complaints from the occupant of the next apartment, until she learned who was making "those awful repetitive noises," and would join us in the evening. One day Jack Hammond and I started to take Leonore and Ira to the crypt of the Capuchin church to see the tombs of all the Hapsburgs. But there was one of those delightful open-air cafes opposite the church and we sat there all afternoon discussing whether George should continue on Broadway or go symphonic and never paid our respects to the

174

Hapsburgs. Another day we went to a ceremonious "tea" lasting from five until about ten, given by Frau Johann Strauss, the aged widow of the Waltz King. She was a fascinating old lady, full of anecdotes about her husband, Rubinstein, Liszt, Tschaikowsky and many other great names which seemed too far in the past for even her living memory. We asked with bated breath about Brahms but she complained that his music was too modern for her approval, that it held no musical beauty and dismissed him as "just a Hamburger." There was obviously more behind her terse remarks than met the eye and ear, but it seemed a remarkable way to kick genius off Olympus. Before we left she tried to sell us the manuscript of *Die Fledermaus,* for quite a healthy sum, but our enjoyment of the afternoon did not reach that peak.

A year later I heard *An American in Paris* twice in one evening in Boston. George was there for the tryout of *Show Girl,* which he'd written for Ziegfeld, and asked me to dinner and to hear Casella conduct *The American* at Symphony Hall and then dash to the Colonial Theatre to hear it incorporated as a ballet in *Show Girl.* Vienna had proved an excellent workshop. It was fascinating in both guises and will surely live with the *Rhapsody,* the *Concerto* and *Porgy and Bess* as one of George's "Big Four" contributions to music.

George spent a weekend that summer at Jack Hammond's Gothic Castle in Gloucester, near Boston. It is a fabulous place, containing a Great Hall of stone, 100 feet long by 70 feet high, arched like a cathedral transept, in which all forms of music sound richer than in any room of my experience. Hammond had continued his favorite avocation of acoustic development, from the piano to the phonograph, and was then perfecting an amazing system of amplification through thirty loud-speakers scat-

175

tered high in the tower of the Great Hall. He produced, merely from the ordinary records one buys, the most inspiring music I have ever heard. Stokowski, Koussevitzky and all the leading conductors and soloists had heard their work exalted by this mysterious device but it remained for George to add a new touch. He played his *Rhapsody* on Hammond's amplified piano with the accompaniment of his records on the amplified orthophonic and the result was sensational. George's phenomenal musical zest became even accelerated and we literally stayed up all night, experimenting with new controls and trying new combinations of sound made possible by shifting a lever here and there. It was an exciting, memorable evening.

Next day the word spread that Gershwin was staying at Hammond's and various hostesses telephoned from Manchester, Pride's Crossing and even Boston, asking if they might bring their dinner guests in for music, with the result that over a hundred people descended on us and George had to play the *Rhapsody,* the *Concerto* and parts of *An American in Paris* with this dramatic accompaniment until three in the morning. Madame Nazimova, invited to spend a quiet, restful weekend in the country after a trying week of appearing in *The Cherry Orchard* in Boston, arrived at midnight and fled to her room and remained invisible until luncheon next day. The last evening of his visit George entertained us with his well-known stories about his beloved father, the radio yarn about "Cuba guaranteed" being especially amusing to our host, of radio fame. He played all the numbers from his forthcoming *Girl Crazy,* and a musically vivid weekend closed with a repetition of the *Rhapsody* under these unique conditions and echoes of dynamic sound ringing through the Great Hall.

Later weekends in California come to mind, at the beautiful ranch home of Mr. and Mrs. Sidney Fish in Carmel, where the atmosphere of earlier years at their hospitable home on Long Island was duplicated, and where George indulged in his favorite game of golf at the Cypress Point Club. Always interested in the other arts, he discussed painting, his preferred avocation, with Francis McComas and Paul Dougherty, and poetry with Robinson Jeffers as intelligently as his favorite music. It seems a strange coincidence that his last visit there was only a few weeks before the death of our great mutual friend, Mrs. Fish, and but two months before his own.

Back in New York in 1934 I recall an unusually gay evening in honor of Noel Coward at Mrs. Frances Wellman's apartment at the Waldorf. Her rare talent as a hostess was responsible for our hearing George Gershwin, Cole Porter, Irving Berlin, Noel Coward, Rodgers and Hart, and Dwight Fiske all perform their latest successes in one evening, with Yvonne Printemps singing delightfully and Elsa Maxwell furnishing some robust piano playing. George was just completing *Porgy and Bess* and succeeded amazingly in giving us an intriguing idea of that complex score merely with his two hands and his inelastic voice. He seemed able to give the complete illusion of orchestra, solo voices and chorus, describing the action as well, while the additional accompaniment of the long black cigar never interfered with his brother Ira's lyrics.

I heard *Porgy and Bess* in its entirety only a few weeks ago in Los Angeles. Its magnificent choral passages surging from pathos to power, its revelation of Gershwin the musical dramatist, the entire work impressed me, far more than elaborate tributes, as the greatest and most significant memorial possible to George Gershwin, the "Happy Prince" of music, whose lamentably brief career never knew the staleness of anticlimax.

177

1937·ERMA TAYLOR

Like wailing, weeping notes they were, the autumn leaves, as they sighed and swept about me when I wended my way to his last home. And when I went into the shaded, hushed room whence the last echo of his playing had long since ceased, and saw the silent piano — with the pad of unscored pages "Printed for George Gershwin" still waiting upon the music rack — the cascading leaves cast pale shadow cadences across the white sheets, and I witnessed Nature composing her own inaudible Lament for George Gershwin . . .

With Nature we mourn his passing, for the years will be many before we stop listening for new melodies from him whom we hailed as our defender—our prophet—our promise to the music of the ages. We too lament, because we know he left so many songs yet unsung.

The world's favorite artist is the composer, for his gift knows no boundaries of race, place, language nor time. Melody and rhythm and harmony are universal, of all times and all people, and with these as his warp and his woof and his design, the composer weaves his enchantment. The composer is international and immortal, for at any time any musician can reproduce the magic he wove.

And so it was with George Gershwin. We hold him especially dear, because he was one of us, and while others heard only the discordant pandemonium of our times he listened for the overtones from which he captured the ecstasies and sorrows, the gaiety and melancholy, the dance and the dirge that comprise the inarticulate hubbub that is so definitely America. He was our melodic spokesman, and not only did he win the world's approval for *musica americana,* but more important to us, he justified us to ourselves. He bridged the chasm between jazz and the symphony, and he brought the opera to the people. He made peace between the dance hall and the concert stage, the movie palace and the opera house. He democratized music, and he was the idol of that new democracy. None before him accomplished so much. No other composer has been so versatile.

In a certain sense, those who best knew George Gershwin mourn him least. This is because those intimates who were privileged to know George as well as Gershwin realize that not a single regret clings about his bier. They know that few if any men ever lived as fully, as harmoniously, as exultantly, as masterfully as young Gershwin—and knowing this, there can scarcely be room for sorrow in their hearts.

Just as his music was heedless of traditions, so was his life anomalous to the life patterns one expects of composers. His story runs much truer to the Horatio Alger idyl. The typical composer is emaciated, poverty-stricken, melancholy, wild-eyed, introverted, misunderstood, unwept. Gershwin was vigorously healthy, wealthy, gay, affable, extroverted, beloved . . . and no composer before him has been so honored in death.

George was an agile sportsman, skilled at golf, tennis, ping-pong, fishing and wrestling. There was an elaborate gymnasium in his New York penthouse. His average income the last decade was $250,000—a quarter of a million dollars—a year. He was a thoroughly happy person, understanding and enjoying his fellowman and himself. He loved parties, especially when he officiated at the keyboard. He liked people, and his swanky modernistic penthouse atop a seventeen-story apartment building on Riverside Drive was the rendezvous and salon of the creators and interpreters of the New York world of arts. Many of the guests swarming continually in and out of his apartment were unknown to their host, but George could work at his piano in the midst of a riot, and he never refused to see anyone. He remembered all too well how much the encouragement of Irving Berlin and Jerome Kern had meant to his youthful years, and he never forgot any of those who had helped him. He remembered even the dates at which he had met personages who meant much in his life. Accordingly, he gave interviews as generously and graciously to the reporters of high school papers as to the critics of the country's most influential publications.

One of the loveliest memories a visitor carried from the Gershwin ménage was that of the warmth and harmony one sensed between all the Gershwins, for usually all of them lived under one roof. Between Ira and George there was the closest kind of understanding—though opposites in temperament and talents, they worshipped and envied each other's natures. Sister Frances's devotion was pretty well attested when she had George play his *Rhapsody in Blue* at her wedding to Leopold Godowsky. Of their mother, George once said: "My mother's what the mammy writers write about, and what the mammy singers sing about. But they don't mean it; and I do." And then there's the typical story about Papa Gershwin. It seems Papa was exceeding Manhattan's speed limit one day. When the policeman started writing out a ticket, indignant Papa Gershwin protested: "Don't you know who I am? I'm the father of George Gershwin!" Bearing in mind that the Yiddish pronunciation of "George" sounds strangely like "Judge," it's no wonder the cop scratched his head, recon-

180

sidered, and obsequiously apologized. It's been Papa Gershwin's firm conviction ever since that his son's name could open the pearly gates themselves.

And so it could scarcely be said that George was born into a misunderstanding family. It was on September 26, 1898, that George (*ne* Jacob) Bruskin Gershvin let out a birth wail that twenty-four and one-half years later would be echoed by the clarinet glissando of *Rhapsody in Blue*. His parents were Russian Jews from St. Petersburg, where Grandpa Bruskin was a furrier, and Grandpop Gershvin invented guns for the Czar. Papa Gershvin's work is difficult to record, because he was inoculated with the heritage of his people — the wanderlust. Restlessly he tried to find his place in the American scheme of things — as a cobbler, a cigar stand attendant, a bookmaker, as a Turkish bath, billiard parlor and restaurant proprietor. And every time Papa Gershwin changed his business, the Gershwin family moved; as a consequence, his first sixteen years saw George calling twenty-eight tenements home. Yet the Gershwin nomadicism (confined as it was to New York) had its virtues: it made the four young Gershwins adaptable. In each place George readily assumed leadership of the neighborhood gang; perhaps it was because he already possessed the qualifications necessary to popularity—or perhaps it was because in the sidewalk brawls of the Bronx and the Ghetto, George was always the guy on the top of the heap.

What about music? "Humph. Kids that went in fer that stuff wuz nuts, screwy — little Maggies." That's what George thought — that is, that's what he thought till that day at Public School 25 when little Maxie Rosenzweig (now renowned as Max Rosen) gave a recital during recess. Of course George didn't attend the recital—who'd listen when he could play baseball instead?—but the violin strains of *Humoresque* floated through the assembly walls, and suddenly George's interest in the ball game waned.

"It was, to me, a flashing revelation of beauty. I made up my mind to get acquainted with Maxie, and waited outside from three to four-thirty. It was pouring cats and dogs by then, and I got soaked to the skin. No luck. I found out where he lived, and dripping wet as I was, trekked to his house, unceremoniously presenting myself as an admirer. Maxie had left. His family was so amused, however, that a meeting was arranged. From the first moment we became the closest of friends—we cut school together, wrestled together—and eternally we talked music. Maxie opened the world of music to me, and he nearly closed it, too. He wasn't at all kind to my budding ambitions. And there came a climactic day when he told me flatly that I had better give up all thought of a musical career. 'You haven't it in you, Georgie; take my word for it, I can tell'!"

Thus did Max Rosen introduce George to music. Thereafter older brother Ira was immediately crowded off the stool of the new piano Mama Gershwin had bought "because my aunt had one," and at the age of twelve George Gershwin had found his work, his religion, himself. There were several teachers, among whom Charles Hambitzer was most important. Hambitzer recognized in the youngster's enthusiasm and precocious ability a musical genius. And the student worshipped his teacher. The days between lessons were an eternity to George, and once there, the clock was never consulted. Hambitzer came of a musical dynasty, and the wealth of all his background was relayed to his favorite pupil. Hambitzer died of tuberculosis at thirty-seven—but one year younger than George when brain tumor overtook him. George never had another regular teacher, and

182

with the loss of his maestro, his pianistic ambitions also died. After Hambitzer, most of George's musical education was self-taught, and he was ever an assiduous student of things musical. At the time of his death he was studying Shillinger's Symmetrical Forms, which look like a geometrical maze to the layman. As a boy he studied theory books and the scores of other composers, but primarily he listened. He sold tickets to the musical programs of New York for the privilege of listening. And he listened not only with his ears, but with his nerves, his mind, his heart. He saturated himself in the music . . . and then he went home and listened in memory. By ear he recreated the motifs on his own piano. He made what he had heard his own, by memorizing, and then by improvising variations around the original themes. He had a memory, and he had originality. He knew where he was going, and he was on his way.

At fifteen, George turned professional, as a piano pounder in the plugging department of Remick's. At $15 a week—a fortune to an East Sider but a year out of grammar school in 1913. And he was "in" Tin Pan Alley. He got paid for playing the music of Kern and Berlin. Their rhythms set his blood racing. Eagerly he imitated and experimented himself, but when he presented his embryonic compositions to the bosses, he was reminded "We hired a piano player—not a writer." Just the same it was excellent discipline. It taught George to transpose at sight, and it gave him ten hours of piano practice a day. It taught him what failed and what clicked with the public. And it taught him the limitations of popular music—music written, for the most part, by comparatively illiterate tunesmiths whose musical abilities were limited to the agility of one finger. That wasn't George's idea of composing; he wanted to compose more than the melody —the harmonies, the arrangements, every last note must be his, too.

He became restless. He had met Berlin, and Berlin encouraged him. On holidays he stood outside Kern's window, too timid to knock and present himself to his god, content just to listen to the spasmodic strains of the composer at work. By now his idols had shifted from virtuosi to composers; henceforth the piano would be a means rather than an end. And at Remick's, George was given no opportunity to compose. He had stuck it out three years; he must gamble on his creative talents. But where to turn? Berlin offered to double his Remick salary in exchange for secretarial services, but agreed acceptance would be inadvisable. George should remain on his own. He seemed to know only what not to do.

Kern wrote musicals; George would get himself connected with musicals. He sold one song, *When You Want 'Em You Can't Get 'Em, When You've Got 'Em You Don't Want 'Em* (lyrics by Murray Roth), but his profits totaled just $5. So he became rehearsal pianist for Ziegfeld's *Miss 1917*. At a Sunday night "concert" Vivienne Segal introduced two of his numbers; Max Dreyfus signed Composer Gershwin at $35 a week. Dreyfus was the discoverer of Kerns, Youmans and Rodgers; he knew how to handle composers. "I'll gamble on you. I'll give you $35 a week, without any set duties. Just step in every morning and say 'Hello.' The rest will follow." The "rest" started with *You-oo, Just You, Some Wonderful Sort of Someone,* and *I Was So Young, You Were So Beautiful,* among others, used as interpolations in musicals. George's name was actually on the sheet music—"Music by George Gershwin." Maxie Rosenzweig was wrong—he did have it in him.

1919 brought George's first complete score to Broadway, *La La Lucille.* It also ushered in *Swanee,* which flopped at the Capitol; nine months later Jolson heard and adopted it for his spectacle, *Sinbad.* A failure turned overnight into a hit. 2,250,000 phonograph records alone were sold throughout the U. S.; two years later it was still the rage in London. Thereafter Gershwin's was a meteoric rise. Beginning in 1920, he wrote *George White's Scandals* music for five consecutive years. Between 1920 and 1930 twenty-five complete Gershwin musicals appeared, beside innumerable independent hits, the score for one picture, the *Rhapsody in Blue, Concerto in F, Preludes* and *An American in Paris.*

And in the midst of all this prolificacy, George led a completely normal and joyous personal life. There were parties almost nightly. Everywhere he was welcomed and fawned upon. Yet George remained his naïve self, ever appreciative of praise, ever grateful and thrilled by small favors. He was never a person to take things or people for granted. He had an abundant capacity, a talent for enjoying life. And he developed his hobby to such a fine point that it approached a career in itself. For like most true geniuses, Gershwin was versatile. Had he not been a musician, art critics acknowledge he would have been one of our leading artists; Merle Armitage puts him on a par with many of our contemporary masters of pen and pencil sketching. His oil and pen portraits have frequently been exhibited. He was also an ardent and extravagant collector. And as Einstein is more pleased with a compliment on his violin playing than with a salute to his mathematical reputation, as Kreisler gets a greater thrill from showing his library of rare literary editions than from exhibiting his violins, as Leonardo was more proud of his repute as a physicist than his prowess as a painter, so Gershwin was more proud of his picture gallery than of his musicianship.

Many people, especially women, wondered why Gershwin never married, and no one wondered more than George himself. Women fascinated him, and surely he envied Ira his happy marriage. He wanted to marry—and yet, he could never bring himself to the actual step. It bothered him so much that he consulted a psychoanalyst about it: there was some vague explanation about his perfectionism—George put women on a pedestal, said the analyst, and when they inevitably failed to possess all the attributes he admired in all women, he was disillusioned in the individual. When he was teased about his perennial bachelorhood, he pointed laughingly at his long life line, and protested he had years yet in which to marry. I don't know that he actually believed in palmistry, but the mysticism inevitable in an intuitive creator like George Gershwin cannot altogether disregard nor scoff at psychic phenomena. And if George's long life line gave him a certain reassurance, it was a fortuitous deception. For George never realized how ill he was—he never doubted but what there were a million melodies yet to come.

His friends' fondest memories are of George at the piano, with the ubiquitous cigar, a joyous smile on his lips and in his eyes, his powerful hands caressing the keys he loved so dearly. And his playing was such that had he not been a composer he would have been famous as a virtuoso of the piano. His appearance with orchestras invariably signified a sell-out of tickets, and in his last years Gershwin was acquiring distinction too as a conductor. Orchestras and impresarios enjoyed working with him—he knew just what effects he wanted, and he knew how to achieve them. Without affectation, without "temperament," but with enthusiastic appreciation for all, his relations with others were always happy. Unfortunately, only his piano *Preludes* and the *Rhapsody in Blue* were ever recorded with George at the piano, and both of these are out of print.

The *Rhapsody* probably had the most interesting background of all

186

Gershwin's works. The story really began back in 1922, when George made a daring experiment in the *Scandals*: he composed a one-act jazz opera entitled *135th Street*. It had a Harlem setting, and gave the composer a chance to dramatize the negro jazz that was sweeping the country. It met a varied reaction: a New Haven critic pronounced "This opera will be imitated in a hundred years"; a Broadway critic reviewed it as "the most dismal, stupid and incredible blackface sketch that has probably ever been perpetrated." But let the critics rant, let George White withdraw it from the show; one man was impressed. Paul Whiteman conducted the *Scandals* orchestra, and he liked it so well that a year later he remembered it when drawing up plans for his famous Aeolian Hall Concert, at which he planned to justify jazz. He suggested that George write something for the concert. But in the fall of 1923 George had commissions for four complete 1924 musicals, beside the début into the musical intelligentsia, *via* the memorable Eva Gauthier recital, for which he was to compose and accompany. The Whiteman Emancipation of Jazz was symbolically scheduled for Lincoln's birthday, 1924. In January George read in the newspaper that he, Gershwin, was at work on a symphonic contribution to the program that Whiteman heralded as the *piece de resistance* of the musical menu. No one was more shocked than George—but who was he to make the newspaper out a liar? He had really decided against doing it, but Aeolian Hall—gosh, that was something! At first he considered a regulation blues number, short, sad and simple. But then:

"Suddenly an idea occurred to me. There had been so much talk about the limitations of jazz, not to speak of the manifest misunderstandings of its function. Jazz, they said, had to be in strict time. It had to cling to dance rhythms. I resolved, if possible, to kill that misconception with one sturdy

187

blow. Inspired by this aim, I set to work composing. I had no set plan, no structure to which my music must conform. The rhapsody, you see, began as a purpose, not a plan. I worked out a few themes, but just at this time I had to appear in Boston for the premiere of *Sweet Little Devil.* It was on the train, with its steely rhythms, its rattlety-bang that is often so stimulating to a composer (I frequently hear music in the very heart of noise) that I suddenly heard—even saw on paper—the complete construction of the rhapsody, from beginning to end. No new themes came to me, but I worked on the thematic material already in my mind, and tried to conceive the composition as a whole. I heard it as a sort of musical kaleidoscope of America—of our vast melting pot, of our incomparable national pep, our blues, our metropolitan madness. By the time I reached Boston I had a definite plot of the piece, as distinguished from its actual substance. The middle theme came upon me suddenly, as my music oftentimes does. It was at the home of a friend, just after I got back to Gotham. I must do a great deal of what you might call subconscious composing, and this is an example. Playing at parties is one of my notorious weaknesses. Well, as I was playing, without a thought of the rhapsody, all at once I heard myself playing a theme that must have been haunting me inside, seeking outlet. No sooner had it oozed out of my fingers than I realized I had found it. Within a week of my return from Boston I had completed the structure, in the rough, of the *Rhapsody in Blue.*"

In that week Whiteman haunted the Gershwin apartment, desperate for the score that was to make or break his reputation. Over Gershwin's protests (for George has never been thoroughly satisfied with the *Rhapsody*) he took the score, unpolished as it was. To Ferde Grofé went the arranging assignment, and Ferde excelled himself . . . although at the concert itself George improvised piano figurations in the solo.

February 12, 1924, arrived. Whiteman, exhausted by nightmares, apprehension, overwork and last minute stage fright, had a terrified impulse to call it all off when he saw Damrosch, Heifetz, Godowsky, Kreisler, McCormack, Rachmaninoff and the highbrow critics actually appearing at the door. He should have been encouraged; it was snowing, yet people were virtually fighting for entrance. There were buyers for ten times the available seats. What Whiteman lost in cash ($7,000—the production cost him $11,000, and there were only $4,000 worth of seats) he regained in publicity. The Sunday papers carried column after column of reviews, some bad, some good, all loquacious, and most of them respectful. The critics sustained their dignity and superiority, of course, by pointing out the *Rhapsody's* technical immaturity as manifest in structural and harmonic weaknesses, but all blushingly or frankly confessed with Sanborn: "The thing certainly has zip and punch." Deems Taylor recognized Gershwin as "a link between the jazz camp and the intellectuals." Damrosch enthused "Gershwin has made a lady out of jazz." All advised that Mr. Gershwin would bear watching. Mr. Gershwin, as a matter of fact, was the hero of the day—and the days and years to follow, for no one, least of all Mr. Gershwin, anticipated the popularity awaiting the *Rhapsody* in America and the even greater welcome it received in Europe.

After the *Rhapsody* George's ambitions knew no limits, and he became aware of his responsibility as America's foremost musical hope. To fulfill the expectations of America's serious musicians, he composed the *Concerto in F,* introduced by Damrosch, and the *Preludes* for the recital platform. The tone-poem, *An American in Paris,* was his answer to those who thought his previous successes lucky accidents. And then George's dreams set upon an opera—an opera of the people. It took several years to find the right book, but in DuBose Heyward's novel *Porgy and Bess* his search ended. With the collaboration of Heyward and brother Ira (who since 1924 had been his chief lyricist), his greatest ambition was undertaken in 1933. Everything else, including the quarter of a million income a year, was dropped. Till long after midnight every night George worked for two long years. He forsook his comfortable apartment to live several months in an humble shack on the waterfront in Charleston. He lost himself in Stephen Foster melodies and negro spirituals. He mulled over operatic forms, and mastered the medieval fugue. But in the main, he consulted with his own intuitive muse, and after eleven months of composition and nine of instrumentation (for Gershwin himself arranged all his works but the *Rhapsody*), he trusted his favorite brainchild to its début before a critical public—a year behind schedule. Quoting George himself:

"*Porgy and Bess* is a folk tale. Its people would naturally sing folk-music. When I first began work on the music I decided against the use of original folk-material, because I wanted the music to be all of one piece. Therefore, I wrote my own spirituals and folk songs. But they are still folk-music, and therefore, being in operatic form, *Porgy and Bess* becomes folk-opera.

"However, because *Porgy and Bess* deals with Negro life in America, it brings to the operatic form elements that have never before appeared in opera, and I have adapted my method to utilize the drama, the humor, the superstition, the religious fervor, the dancing and the irrepressible high spirits of the race. If, in doing this, I have created a new form, which combines opera with theatre, this new form has come quite naturally out of the material."

Surely *Porgy and Bess* fulfilled Gershwin's dreams for it, because it is in effect America's only opera—it's the only American opera accepted by America. It was so successful that it ran almost a year in New York and on tour. Far more important, the public loves it—loves it as the Italians love their opera; one hears it sung on the streets, whistled in offices; Bing Crosby and Lily Pons sing its songs, and every day one hears *Summertime* or *It Ain't Necessarily So* or *I Got Plenty o' Nuttin'* on the radio. By it George would prefer to be judged.

But who can judge George Gershwin? The critics? Critics are trained to find flaws—to concentrate on the weaknesses of a man and his works. And as with the rest of us, their opinions vary—some denounce him roundly, because he entered the world of music *via* the illegitimate heritage of jazz; some unreservedly crown him the John the Baptist of a new musical glory to come. The composers? The composers were his chums, and his rivals; they judge him in the light of the brilliant personality they loved, or their pride jaundices their reactions. The conservatives look upon him as a transitionist, as one whose chief service was the liberation of overly formalized music and the respectable-izer of jazz. As for me, who am I to judge? I only know that when I hear *The Man I Love* my mind ceases judging and I can understand the woman who loves lavishly but indiscreetly; and when I hear the *Rhapsody in Blue* the blood in my veins stops flowing and my heart stands still and I am suspended in a rapture of exaltation; and when I hear *Summertime* my little cares are forgotten, and I am in ecstatic harmony and in love with the whole world.

It is not for us to judge. The years will do that . . . and if the present tendency is significant, we need not worry about the years' leniency with George Gershwin, for the popularity of even his early songs is still growing. His music simply is not dated. We have never tired of *I Got Rhythm*

191

nor *Bidin' My Time* nor *The Man I Love,* of the *Rhapsody in Blue* nor *An American in Paris.* They are as fresh, as invigorating today as the day he wrote them.

And it really matters not what the critics say about his music. For we know that what the Fathers of our country did for our nation George Gershwin did for music. He democratized music . . . and is it any wonder he was the idol of that democracy?

No composer before him was ever so much beloved by his own time, for few are the pioneers—especially of music—who live to see their contributions recognized. Yet Gershwin accomplished all this in so brief a span of years that his mother and grandmother outlived him to hear the greatest of all Memorial Concerts broadcast in his honor 'round all the world.

1938·EVA GAUTHIER

Two things lie before me. One is George's last letter from Hollywood, dated March 17, 1937, expressing his regret that he could not be in New York to play for me the famous group of songs we did together in 1923 (a concert which made musical history but was never repeated and now, alas, never will be). The American program was to be a continuation of my series of retrospective programs given by me last season and postponed until the fall of 1937 when he would be back in New York. The other is a clipping from the *New York Times*:

"George Gershwin and Hector Villa Lobos (Brazil) have been elected honorary members of the Academy of Santa Cecilia, Rome. The Appointees to the Academy Board include Pizzetti and Tommasini (two of Italy's composers who rank with the foremost of our time). The board includes almost all of the important European composers."

Now let me go back fourteen years—such a short time ago—and quote, from the *Literary Digest* of November 24, 1923, a summary of a review by Deems Taylor of a New York concert at Aeolian Hall, November 4, 1923, at which George Gershwin accompanied me in a group of songs of his own composition, and others by Irving Berlin, Jerome Kern and Walter Donaldson.

"A pause. The singer reappeared, followed by a tall, black-haired young man who was far from possessing the icy aplomb of those to whom playing on the platform of Aeolian Hall is an old story. He bore under his arm a small bundle of sheet music with lurid black and red and yellow covers. The audience began to show signs of relaxation; this promised to be amusing . . . Young Mr. Gershwin began to do mysterious and fascinating rhythmic and contrapuntal stunts with the accompaniment . . . by the time *Swanee* arrived he (a famous European musician, previously mentioned) was having as shamelessly good a time as anybody, and when the singer had finished she faced a new audience."

The Gershwin songs used that evening were *Stairway to Paradise, Innocent Ingenue Baby* (written in collaboration with William Daly, now also dead), the famous *Swanee* and, as an encore, *Do It Again.*

In the audience was Paul Whiteman, who had then reached the peak of success as the leader of the finest dance orchestra in the country, and he decided there and then that he too could give an Aeolian Hall concert with his band, and came back stage to ask George to write him something for his orchestra, with a piano part which George might play. This, when completed, was the *Rhapsody in Blue,* performed for the first time on February 12, 1924, in Aeolian Hall.

After our concert, a jazz party was given by Mary Opdyke (now Mrs. John DeWitt Peltz). This was George's first introduction to New York society, to which he was to be, from then on, such a brilliant addition and attraction. In the meantime he was busy with a revue for London and with several other things. As I had decided to repeat our concert in Boston late in January, 1924, we started to re-rehearse our now famous group of songs, as George wanted to improve the accompaniments. I had fully convinced him at last of the importance of this commission and persuaded him to turn his attention to it in earnest.

In the days just before leaving for Boston as we rehearsed our group for that concert he would bring and play for me the developed themes of the new work. I met Olin Downes, who had just arrived in New York from Boston to take up his new post of music editor of the *New York Times,* and he was very disappointed at having missed the concert here. As he was unable to attend the one to be given in Boston I invited him to attend the last rehearsal, along with other friends who wished to hear and meet Gershwin again. (The New York concert had been reviewed by Mr. Scholes of the *London Times,* who had been here as guest critic of the *New York Times.*) Arthur Bliss, the famous English composer, was also there as I had included a group of his new songs on the New York program which were to be repeated in Boston. It was so interesting to see how Gershwin was already outstanding with his personality and talent and able to hold his own against such a competitor as Bliss. Later Bliss played for me in California several concerts at which Gershwin's songs were featured, and I must admit that although I missed the support of the real jazz player, George's songs, nevertheless, stood out.

When we were through the rehearsal I asked Gershwin to play his new work for our small and selected audience and see what their reaction would be. When he was asked what it was he replied, "Oh, just a new work for Paul Whiteman's concert in a few days, if I can get it finished in time." And that was really the first performance of the *Rhapsody in Blue.* It is thrilling to think that we heard in creation a work that has played such a vital rôle in the development of American musical expression and musical ideas.

The Boston concert was just as exciting as the New York one. Amy Lowell, in her autobiography, speaks about the concert and of meeting

Gershwin afterward at a party given for us. She has reproduced in her book a letter to me repeating how much she felt that it was an occasion to be remembered.

Then came London in 1925. Just before leaving we were engaged to go to Derby, Connecticut, and give a repetition of the New York and Boston concerts. The reason why I mention this concert is that the first performance of *The Man I Love* was given in Derby; written originally for *Lady Be Good,* but withdrawn for the lack of some one able to sing it, the song was used several years later in the first version of *Strike Up The Band.* This song was popular in Europe before it became a hit in America, and is now considered one of his best songs. He loved to sing it himself and did it in a most delightful way. I believe that it will always be popular, and really in time become a folk song.

There was another occasion for great excitement just before leaving for London—Walter Damrosch commissioned George to write a work for a symphony orchestra which was the piano *Concerto in F* for which he did his own orchestration. (Ferde Grofé had orchestrated *Rhapsody in Blue* as there had not been time for Gershwin to do it for the Whiteman concert.)

After our London concert, which was a repetition of the New York and Boston programs, Lord and Lady Carisbrooke (cousins of King George V) gave a party for us. It was Gershwin's first meeting with royalty and it was as if he had always belonged there. With his charm and talent he made the party alive and interesting and had everyone around the piano as he sang and played all his latest songs and dance hits.

But our London concert raised a terrific controversy, especially with Ernest Newman, the great English critic, who could not make up his mind about it. He could not deny that he had got a "kick" out of Gershwin's music and I know that he had later to admit that the *Rhapsody in Blue* was well worth re-hearing and showed tremendous talent. But it was too much of a jolt for the English—too radical an innovation in the concert hall. It took nine recitals before I could make them forgive me.

The famous Whiteman concert presenting the *Rhapsody in Blue,* with Gershwin at the piano, was repeated (after its first performance at Aeolian Hall) in Carnegie Hall for a benefit concert to raise funds for a fellowship in composition at the American Academy in Rome. What a triumph Gershwin enjoyed, both as composer and as pianist! The audience included many of the greatest musicians—Paderewski, Rachmaninoff and Leopold Auer—in fact, every one of any note was there to applaud and cheer the newcomer and he was forced to repeat the entire work. After that followed the performance of the concerto commissioned by Damrosch for the New York Symphony and the *Second Rhapsody* commissioned by Koussevitsky for the Boston Symphony. I had the thrill of hearing all of these works in the making, with George singing the orchestra part and playing the piano part in the inimitable way in which he could do these things. Other evenings stand out at the home of the late Paul Kochanski, the great Polish violinist, when Gershwin played the new songs for the coming "shows" and enthralled us all with the joy of life and of his music, singing and playing and getting our reaction to the new "show numbers," as he called them.

In 1928 in Paris he played for me his then latest composition, *An American in Paris,* which he wrote there. I think he was a little depressed and homesick, as this composition evidences a nostalgia of New York, even though he is describing his impressions of Paris with its gaiety and

197

all the new impressions of a new country and new people and his contact with the young French composers, to whom he pays tribute in his own way, just as later on Ravel was to pay tribute to Gershwin in his last work written after his American visit.

In London he became the good friend of Prince George, now the Duke of Kent, who used to drop in at George's apartment while he played to him. Gershwin took great pride in a photograph inscribed "To George from George." But with all this adulation and success he never lost his simplicity and it never turned his head. On acquiring his first apartment at 33 Riverside Drive he gave a housewarming, and at his first dinner party his guests were all those who had helped him in the beginning of his career. The place cards written by George were bars of music from his most successful song hits—mine was *The Man I Love*. Among the guests, I remember Professor Auer, Ernest Hutcheson, Mr. Dreyfuss, his publisher, Paul Whiteman, Ferde Grofé, Adele and Fred Astaire, Walter Damrosch, William Daly, and, of course, his brother Ira. The devotion between the brothers was a very rare one and they always lived near to one another.

Paul Whiteman told that evening of the agonies of the first performance of the *Rhapsody,* for which Gershwin had not had time to write out the piano part—he had just indicated the number of bars. In fact, some of it was heard for the first time at that performance. He proved himself at this concert to have an outstanding pianistic talent, with a formidable technique, and later took his place with the other great pianists of his time.

In the later years Gershwin began to paint, showing much talent with the brush, and he also began to acquire a very important collection of modern paintings which were loaned from time to time to various important exhibitions at which also his own works were shown. Before leaving for California he loaned his entire collection to the Museum of Modern Art. It would be a fine thing if this collection were kept permanently on display in his memory. It is one of my deep regrets that we never managed to get around to the portrait of myself that he wanted to paint.

In 1927, when the late Maurice Ravel came to this country, one of his wishes was to meet Gershwin, hear the *Rhapsody, The Man I Love,* and see one of his "shows," all of which I was able to arrange. The show was *Funny Face* with the Astaires, which enchanted Ravel. The two met at a dinner which I gave to celebrate Ravel's fifty-third birthday, and after dinner Gershwin played the *Rhapsody* and, in fact, his entire repertoire, and fairly outdid himself. It was an unforgetable evening, the meeting of the two most outstanding composers of the day, the young man just beginning to scale the heights, the other at the very pinnacle. (That was before the *Bolero.*) Gershwin was very anxious to work with Ravel, but the answer was that it would probably cause him to write bad "Ravel" and lose his great gift of melody and spontaneity. The thing that astonished Ravel was the facility with which George scaled the most formidable technical difficulties and his genius for weaving complicated rhythms and his great gift of melody. I had to act as interpreter in their conversation, a most interesting task. In Ravel's last big work, the piano concerto, one recognizes the influence of the *Rhapsody in Blue* in some of the effects that are introduced, some of which have now become easily recognized "clichés."

Now for *Porgy and Bess.* Over two years was given to the composing of that work, and I heard it in all its stages. There was a time when he became so exhausted that he stopped for several months and refused to continue the work until he was rested, and so delayed the production one season. The score is beyond doubt one of the finest things he has done. From the time of the *Concerto in F* he did all of his own orchestration and his growth in this part of his work was what was so interesting—a growth which, of course, for the most part, the layman is unable to judge. His actual finished scores were works of art, beautifully bound, and George was very proud to show them to his friends. Just before the opening of *Porgy and Bess* he had a birthday party and I gave him a first edition of the Malipiero realization of the *Orfeo* of Monteverdi (1600). As a dedication, I wrote "The first opera ever written, to the composer of the latest opera." It was a joy to see the pleasure that that gift and the dedication had given him.

The brilliant first night of *Porgy and Bess* is unforgetable. How unfortunate that the Metropolitan did not produce this work to complete its record of the most important of American operas. Alas, to conform with Broadway, many cuts had to be made and some of the best material left out. It was, nevertheless, a superb achievement for our young composer. After the performance a party was given by Mr. Condé Nast, to which all of New York came to pay homage to George Gershwin. Whiteman brought his orchestra and played the *Rhapsody in Blue,* with George playing the piano part. A large silver tray inscribed by all of his friends was presented. The entire cast of *Porgy and Bess* repeated the highlights of the opera.

Gershwin was always willing to help other artists and musicians and many of the young people who have recently become successful were materially aided by his generosity. One is Vladimir Dukelsky, known on Broadway as Vernon Duke, composer of *April in Paris* and a number of other hits, but whose works have been performed by the major symphony orchestras and whose ballets have been performed by Diaglieff and others. Dukelsky finished the uncompleted works of Gershwin for the movies on which he was working at the time of his death. Another is Alexander Steinert (Prix de Rome) whose works also have been performed by the major symphony orchestras, and who conducted all the rehearsals for *Porgy and Bess* and the performances on the road, and is now conducting the work in a revival out on the "Coast." These two musicians learned from him the art of writing for Broadway, and he learned from them the serious side of composition. José Iturbi and his sister are playing with outstanding success a two-piano version of the *Rhapsody in Blue*.

It is futile to attempt to describe in words the shock that the death of this young man was to those who knew him. I had been reassured by his mother that Walter Winchell's reports were exaggerated. She had just returned from Hollywood and said that he was very tired; that he missed all of his New York friends, the music and his paintings, and that he was coming back to New York as soon as he had finished work on his latest motion picture. He did come back, but not for these things, alas.

I have lost a very dear friend; America has lost one of her most talented sons, who made life a little gayer and the world a happier place with his joyous songs and enchanting dance rhythms. He had not said all that he had to say—George Gershwin will live as long as music lives, through his recordings, the radio and orchestras. That is the compensation of the composer, alas denied to the interpreter. He will never be forgotten and his place will never be filled. He will live as the voice of the 20th Century in America in music and the American "Johann Strauss." I am proud of the honor of having given him his first chance to appear both as pianist and composer and to have been his first interpreter on a serious program along with other great contemporary composers of the day. On that famous program of November, 1923, was also the first American performance of the great *Monologue* of the *Gurrelieder* by the great Arnold Schönberg. Years later when as an exile from Germany Schönberg came to America to teach in a Boston School of Music, amongst the fellowships established was one given by George Gershwin enabling a young composer to work with the great teacher (Schönberg's book on composition and harmony being one of the finest in existence). The last year of George's life which he spent in California and where he died, had also become the home of Schönberg. The two became very great friends, both being ardent tennis players; and one of George's last works in painting is a superb Portrait of Arnold Schönberg. What extraordinary tricks fate plays in our lives. The unknown Gershwin of 1923 helping out the great Schönberg in 1933.

So Hail and Farewell to a great composer, pianist, painter, good friend and a delightful host! They say "Whom the gods love, die young." He had more than his share of talent, and I hope the *Stairway to Paradise* was there to guide him on his way to the "Great Beyond."

DAVID
1938·EWEN

It is hard for me to believe that Gershwin is dead, not only because his death came with such suddenness, but also because he died leaving with me the conviction that his best work was yet to come. His last serious work, the opera, *Porgy and Bess,* was so marked an advance—from the point of view of both integration of form and self-assurance in artistic expression—from the larger works that preceded it, that it seemed certain that Gershwin was advancing towards greater creative achievements.

I now recall that the last time I met George Gershwin was at one of the first performances of *Porgy and Bess.* He was standing in the back of the theatre, dressed in an ordinary tweed suit, and—as was almost habitual with him—sadly in need of a shave. I had not seen him for quite some time, and he greeted me with his usual warmth of feeling, told me of things of mine which he had read and liked since we last met, and then asked me what I thought of his opera. I told him what I honestly felt, that to me *Porgy and Bess* represented a considerable advance over the *Rhapsody in Blue* and the *Piano Concerto,* that it appeared to me to be the most maturely conceived large work that he had thus far given us. "Now, George," I remember telling him, "you are really beginning." "I think so, too," George answered laughingly.

It seems impossible now to realize that with *Porgy* Gershwin had really finished.

I have known George Gershwin, have met him at periodic intervals both at his home and in theatres during rehearsals of his shows, for a period spanning a little more than a decade. I have, therefore, personally watched him soar in importance from a comparatively unimportant, though respected and well-paid craftsman of Tin Pan Alley, to a position of first importance in American music—not to mention a position of great wealth and esteem. It has always been to me a source of endless admiration to notice with what a level head he accepted his phenomenal meteoric rise to success. His inherent simplicity and lack of ostentation never deserted him, even with adulatory praise ringing perpetually in his ears. Never did he assume poses of grandeur or self-importance. For example, he never attempted to forget conveniently that his origins stemmed from the slums of New York, nor did he ever separate himself from close associations which he had had before he became famous. Frequently, in gatherings of glittering society, he spoke about his boyhood days on Grand Street when his only contact with music was the weekly piano lesson which he took from a half-deaf and gray-haired maestro who charged him twenty-five cents. In the same way, when he moved in the highest musical circles, he did not assume a pose of false dignity; speaking to Strawinsky or Ravel he was the same George Gershwin of Tin Pan Alley that his friends knew and loved.

He was proud of and devoted to his parents, who were simple middle-class people; and he always had them move in his own society. For his mother, he always held a particularly touching adoration. She is a soft-eyed, little, gentle woman whose entire life rotated about George's many triumphs as a composer. She was always to be found in a prominent seat at important first performances of Gershwin's works, and at the end of the performance she was traditionally the first from whom he accepted congratulations. At his cocktail parties or midnight affairs at his apartment, she was often an honored guest, moving with dignity and respect (Yiddish accent and all) among the celebrities. "You know," George used to tell his friends, "my mother is the sort of woman for whom composers write mammy-songs. Only—*I* mean them."

Several writers on Gershwin have described him as "ingenuous." This has never appeared to me to be a particularly happy or accurate description. For it was not innocence but wisdom that brought Gershwin that unassuming simplicity which was so often interpreted as naïveté. There was, for example, his attitude towards his own music. I know that, even with the acclaim of the entire music-world thundering at his doorstep, he was never quite convinced of his artistic importance. He liked his *Rhapsody in Blue* and the *Concerto* with the adoration of a proud father, delighting in playing portions of them for anyone or everyone who would listen. But his adoration never quite succeeded in blurring the clarity of his critical perception. He knew that his technical equipment was deplorably inadequate. Time and again he spoke to me of retiring from Broadway and devoting himself to serious music study—very much with the same hopeless, day-dreaming air of a clerk speaking of escaping from his work to write a novel or a play. He often felt that, for all his talent, he was little more than a creator of popular songs—charming, ingenious, often brilliantly original popular songs, perhaps—but only popular songs, nevertheless.

When once I told him that I thought his song *The Man I Love* the greatest song composed by an American, he thanked me quietly and then added (it was impossible not to recognize his sincerity!) that he would gladly exchange his wealth and fame if he could possess the ability to compose songs like the *Ave Maria* or *Ständchen* of Franz Schubert instead of Tin Pan Alley successes. At another occasion, he told me of a remark which Otto H. Kahn had made to him about his music. "You are enormously talented, George"—I am, of course, quoting Kahn freely—"and one of the most gifted American composers alive. But you will never be a great composer, George, because you have never really known tragedy and pain." "Do you think that he has hit the nail squarely on the head?" Gershwin asked me. Upon still another occasion, I told Gershwin that I did not like *An American in Paris,* which appeared to me too episodic in treatment and too flabby in form. At first, he attempted to change my opinion by playing for me parts of the work on the piano, and then by performing for me the work on phonograph records. Then, he stopped the second side of the first record in the middle, and impatiently and abruptly said: "I guess you are right, after all."

The truth is that Gershwin was altogether incapable of evaluating his own importance. He looked upon his songs as so much musical slumming on his part, and expected to reach artistic significance only in larger and more pretentious forms. As a matter of fact, he was most important in his less pretentious works. He knew he was not a great composer, nor destined for immortality. It was also difficult for him to believe that he was an important one—even more important than other composers who were much more competent than he.

I have frequently written—and as recently as my latest book—that Gershwin's shortcomings as a composer are formidable. I do not intend to underestimate Gershwin's weakness merely because I am writing an obituary. In the *Rhapsody in Blue,* the *Concerto for Piano and Orchestra* and *An American in Paris,* there are appalling streaks of immaturity and stretches of fumbling technique which must doom these works to an early obscurity. In the larger works, Gershwin could never quite free himself from his stifling sense of inferiority and his embarrassing self-consciousness. He was always aware that he was travelling in territory too expansive for his strength. In all of these large works, therefore, there is present hesitancy and groping. There are, to be sure, moments of gorgeous music—moments when his melodic genius erupts a flow of rich lyricism, moments of inescapably seductive vitality and youth—but these moments are never well coördinated into a unified composition. His large works remain patches of excellent passages.

Yet, Gershwin had his place—a far more important place than he himself felt—both as a musical influence and as an artistic creator. As an influence he has given shape and direction to American music, more so than any other American composer I can think of at the moment. He has evolved an American musical vocabulary which has become a part and parcel of America's self-expression. He literally discovered, alone and un-aided, the artistic possibilities of jazz which he exploited fully. The *Rhapsody in Blue,* with the very first slide of the clarinet, emancipated jazz from the slums—and with such success that, before long, such respected masters of musical composition as Strawinsky, Ravel, Krenek and Kurt Weill were following his banner.

As a creator, his canvas was a limited one—particularly before *Porgy and Bess*—but by no means negligible. In songs, smaller pieces for the piano, and in spasmodic pages of the large works, he could rise to lyric heights achieved by few composers of our day. He had a melodic gift that was heaven-sent—a phenomenal ability to produce an endless variety

207

of gorgeous tunes that avoided the more stereotyped lines of melodic construction. And with it, there was an instinct for rhythm, an exuberance and health of spirit which were his own. Where his lack of technique could not raise insurmountable barriers, as in the song, he could produce music that had distinction and artistic genuineness.

His *Porgy and Bess* was his best work not only because he could here exploit his extraordinary gift for melodic invention in the form of operatic arias, but more especially because he now showed greater self-confidence and poise as a creative artist than ever before. *Porgy and Bess* is not without faults, but despite these faults it remains Gershwin's most satisfying artistic production. Always uniquely gifted in infusing a variety of mood and emotion into the song-form, Gershwin adapted his music to the dramatic requirements of DuBose Heyward's drama with remarkable plasticity. What is even more important is the fact that there is here a unity of purpose; the various melodies are blended into something resembling a coherent artistic design.

It is possible that the opera-form suited Gershwin's gift more gracefully than did the form of the rhapsody, concerto or symphonic-poem. I am inclined to think, however, that the artistic success of *Porgy* does not stem from explanation alone. Of greater pertinence is the fact that *Porgy and Bess* came several years later in Gershwin's development—a full decade after the *Rhapsody in Blue.*

I feel strongly that in *Porgy and Bess,* Gershwin was disclosing new horizons as a composer of serious music, that—had he lived—he would have shown consistent development and growth. And it is this feeling which makes the sting of his passing so much more difficult to bear.

208

1938·ISAMU NOGUCHI

Searching in memory for the face of someone we have known, often requires considerable concentration, especially if asked to describe or draw his picture. In our attempt to give reality to such a person, who may even be our closest friend, we are obliged to call up a duplicate image who talks and acts differently to each of us, yet is our only perception of reality. Imagination can create a particular situation, characteristic gestures, the voice, the place, till suddenly time stops and we are there with our friend in the past.

The timely yet timeless quality of all great art may spring from this very human sense of reality given by the perspective of memory. Let me say that imagination seems to project time so that the present is already a part of history. The past is made alive through art.

In my own work, I have found this true. I have also found that in portrait sculpture it is pleasant to work with other artists for they better understand this necessarily objective attitude. The problem is indeed one of trying to avoid having any opinion whatsoever of the sitter so as to let that image emerge which is as complex and as simple as life.

Such an ideal situation existed when George Gershwin posed for me in 1929. I had barely met him. I neither liked him, nor did I dislike him, as a friend of his recently intimated.

True, like most men, he came rather anxious and antagonistic, though curious. But then neither did he have preconceptions of himself or prejudices in art.

This head remains. An exterior of self assurance verging on conceit does not hide the thoughtfulness of a rich and sensitive nature. I was especially fortunate for I do not believe that at any other time did the impression he created so nearly correspond to what he meant to the world —with the added significance to many of us that he was not only a representative of the twenties but through his music a symbol of our youth. His was that rare gift of being able to transfix in such a slender song as *Oh Lady Be Good* the timely, yet timeless image of an era, poignant still.

Why Gershwin, at the pinnacle of success in an idiom of which he was part and parcel, should yearn for the larger forms of music is quite understandable—his courageous ambition to overcome the limitations of his early training—even his seeming disparagement at times of his native genius. How natural that with all the adulation he received, he felt a responsibility to "deliver" the "great American opera—symphony—ballet." Here was that quality of idealism and striving which raised him far above success—success or failure was immaterial, he was an American, he aspired, he was our own.

That Gershwin also involved himself in the study of painting to the extent that he did, is completely astonishing to me. Did he doubt the adequacy of music as a complete expression, or was it a divertissement? Perhaps fleeing from the exorbitant expectations which are heaped upon genius in the "public eye" painting was his solace.

His deep rooted appreciation of the artist behind art is nowhere better shown than in his interest in collecting their paintings. To him the painting was the artist, their work a study and a joy. He was forever trying to explain such things to his friends.

1929·S. N. BEHRMAN

When I first knew George Gershwin he was living with his family in an apartment in 110th Street. To me, who am forced when I want to write so much as a postcard to shut all doors, cut off the telephone, and cere myself carefully in an immutable silence, it was a perpetual wonder that Gershwin could do his work in the living-room of this particular flat, the simultaneous stamping ground of the other members of the family and the numberless relatives and visitors who would lounge through, lean on the piano, chat, tell stories, and do their setting-up exercises. I have seen Gershwin working on the score of the *Concerto in F* in a room in which there must have been six other people talking among themselves, having tea, and playing checkers. In those days Gershwin used to mumble ineffectually that what he needed was privacy. This mild protest went on for several years and resulted finally in the purchase of a five-story house in West 103rd Street. The top floor was the composer's study; here his treasures were transplanted: the Steinway grand, the "Great Composers Series" drawn for him by Will Cotton, the photograph of Prince George of England informally inscribed "From George to George," the framed poster announcing the performance of the *Concerto* at the Paris Opera, the specially bound scores of Debussy and Wagner. At one time, during those 110th Street days, Gershwin was working simultaneously on the *Concerto* and the scores of *The Song of the Flame* and *Tip-Toes*. During

211

this triple creation he would occasionally emigrate to a suite of rooms in a hotel at Broadway and One Hundredth Street. But even here the "privacy" he achieved was only comparative; here, too, the rooms were generally full of admirers, voluntary secretaries who asked nothing further than to be allowed to copy out a score—and relatives.

The electrical success of the *Rhapsody in Blue* (first played by Paul Whiteman in Aeolian Hall, February 12, 1924) made Gershwin an international figure and the house in 103rd Street, with its presumably sacrosanct top floor, was a symbol of the composer's new dignity.

My last visit to the house in 103rd Street demonstrated vividly the futility of symbols in the face of an overpowering reality. I hadn't seen the Gershwins in a long time and I telephoned to ask if it would be convenient for me to call. It was a sweltering night in September and I arrived at the house about nine o'clock. For a long time I rang the doorbell but got no answer. Through the screened, curtained door-window I could see figures moving inside, and I kept ringing impatiently. No answer. Finally I pushed the door open and walked in. Three or four young men I had never seen before were sitting around the hall smoking. Off the hall was a small reception-room which had been converted into a billiard-room. I peered in—there was a game in progress but I knew none of the players. I asked for George, or his brother Ira. No one bothered to reply, but one of the young men made a terse gesture in the direction of the upper stories. I went up one flight and there I found a new group. One of them I vaguely recognized from 110th Street and I asked him where George and Ira were. He said he thought they were upstairs. On the third floor I found Arthur, the youngest brother, who had just come in and didn't know who was in the house, but on the fourth I got an answer to

212

my—by this time agonized—cry. I heard Ira's voice inviting me up to the fifth. I found him and his wife Leonore trying to keep cool in George's study. I told them of my adventures coming up the stairs. "Who under the sun," I asked, "are those fellows playing billiards on the first floor?"

Ira looked almost guilty. "To tell you the truth," he said, "I don't know!"

"But you must," I insisted. "They looked perfectly at home."

"I really don't," he said. "There's a bunch of fellows from down the street who've taken to dropping in here every night for a game. I think they're friends of Arthur's. But I don't know who they are."

"Where," I demanded sternly, "is George?"

"He's taken his old rooms in the hotel around the corner. He says he's got to a have a little privacy."

And, lest I deduce from this that George had become unbearably temperamental, Ira—who is the fidus Achates of his younger brother as well as his lyricist—added apologetically, "You see, George had to do some work on *Funny Face.*"

As a matter of fact I had long since come to the conclusion that George doesn't in the least need "privacy"—at any rate not for composition. His talent is so amazingly prodigal that he hasn't, like the less favored of us, to dig and prod for it. Possibly his training in Tin Pan Alley when he plugged songs for Remick accustomed him to working under conditions that the average creative artist would find impossible. The *Rhapsody in Blue* was written in a few weeks because he had promised Paul Whiteman a piece for his first concert. The *Concerto in F* was written and scored while he was at work on two musical shows; *An American in Paris,* during a few hectic weeks on the Continent. Mr. Gershwin is

213

thirty; his first show, *La La Lucille,* was produced when he was twenty. Since then he has written thirty full musical scores; three important orchestral works ("*An American in Paris* is the most important American composition since the *Concerto in F*"—I quote from the review written on the morning after the first performance by the music critic of the *World*); a series of piano preludes which, I am told by the same authority, are first-rate; and besides that, literally scores of songs which have never appeared in shows.

Among these last are some of his loveliest. *The Man I Love* was one until it was stuck into the ill-fated *Strike Up the Band.* There was talk once of making up a score of Gershwin's songs which, for one reason or another, had been thrown out of shows, and the list made one feel like going out at once to raise the money. At the mercy of banal librettists and the exigencies of "show business," Mr. Gershwin has to take out songs because the prima donnas can't sing them, or because it's time for the slapstick men, or because they're too intricate for the chorus to dance. Almost anyone who knows him well will tell you that much of his stuff which sounds magnificent when he plays it on the piano is dimmed and muffled by the time it reaches the theatre.

But Gershwin's active repertory at the piano is practically endless; besides the well-known ones, from *Swanee* to *My One and Only* and *Feeling I'm Falling* there is a succession not generally known—among which two prime favorites are the incomparable *Mischa, Jascha, Toscha, Sascha,* written for a party at Jascha Heifetz's, and *My Little Duckie.* It is a seemingly inexhaustible fecundity.

The house in 103rd Street has only recently been abandoned, and Gershwin is installed now in a penthouse apartment in Riverside Drive.

214

To complete the gesture of emancipation, the place is done in ultra-modern style—a rather swooning, Melisandish bedroom, terraced bookshelves and elongated wall-lights in the living-room, and over the dining-room table a weirdly crenellated electric lamp that reminds me somehow of the last act of *Dynamo*. One room, though, is fitted as a gymnasium with old-fashioned punching-bags and fencing-foils.

Personally I regard the break-up of the Gershwin ménage with considerable regret, because it will probably minimize my contacts with Gershwin pére. He is short, rotund, inclined to literalness, and he has that singular and unerring faculty which certain originals have for saying, in any situation, that final thing beyond which there is nothing left to be said. There has accumulated gradually a saga of anecdotes emanating from him; when I meet George or Ira I simply say, "What's the latest?" and I am generally told.

The latest happens to be this. The family was discussing the new Einstein paper and George commented on the astonishing compactness of scientific vocabulary:

"Imagine working for twenty years and putting your results into three pages!"

"Well," said Mr. Gershwin calmly, "it was probably very small print!"

The rest of the family consists of Mrs. Gershwin and a younger brother and sister, Frances and Arthur. Mrs. Gershwin is level-headed and practical; I imagine it was she who steered the family through the early years and who helped Gershwin pére to the eminence of a restaurant proprietor. I gather that it was not her fault that prosperity dwindled in the era immediately before George became famous. When George was

215

growing up the family was so poor it couldn't afford a piano, and it was at some sacrifice that one was secured for him when he was twelve years old. The sister is sporadically on the stage and at Palm Beach, and Arthur does something in the commercial side of films and practices the piano. It is the family joke that one day Arthur will out-distance George, but so far this speculation remains in the region of humor.

This is the background of Gershwin's electrifying genius—a background which has this in common with the environment of most genius —that it remains inscrutable and explains nothing. I use the expression deliberately, for this good-humored, ingenuous young man is one of the most thrilling artists now alive. Because I have no authority to write about music, I have spoken with circumspection of Gershwin's achievements as a composer. I come now to a side of his talent of which I can speak because I have been under its spell—his immediate talent as a pianist, as an interpreter of his own songs. Josef Hofmann says of Gershwin that he has "a fine pianistic talent . . . firm, clear . . . good command over the keyboard." To the layman it seems a positive domination. You get the sense of a complete mastery, a complete authority—the most satisfactory feeling any artist can give you. When he sits at the piano and plays his own songs in a roomful of people, the effect that he evokes is extraordinary. I have seen Kreisler, Zimbalist, Auer, and Heifetz caught up in the heady surf that inundates a room the moment he strikes a chord. It is a feat not only of technique but of sheer virtuosity of personality. At the piano Gershwin takes on a new life and so do his auditors. He sings. He makes elaborate gestures. When he comes to a line in *My Little Ducky*—

Gloria Swanson is hot for me,
Look at the pin she got for me

his hand flies to his tie to convey the better Miss Swanson's magnanimity. Described, this sounds grotesque, but actually it is as beautifully integrated as a clever harmony. Gershwin becomes a sort of sublimated and transplanted troubadour, singing an elemental emotion, an unabashed humor . . .

> Do, do, do what you've done done done before . . .
> Sigh away, cry away, fly away to heaven . . .

Vicariously, you obey. (What a stunt it would be for someone to take a slow movie of a group of people crowded around a piano while Gershwin is playing and run it off without music!) Illuminated and vitalized by his own music, his own voice, his own eager sense of the rhythm of life, Gershwin instantly conveys that illumination and that vitality to others, and that is why he can at once pick up the confused and disparate elements of the average New York party and precipitate them—willy-nilly—into a medium warm and homogeneous and ecstatic.

Of course, Gershwin enjoys his own playing and his own music and his own talent. It is part of the integrity of his effect. There are people who will tell you that Gershwin can't write a tune and there are people who will tell you that he plays too long at parties. There are, in fact, all sorts of people. As a matter of fact, Gershwin has been exploited mercilessly by hostesses—and hosts—whose parties he has saved from irredeemable dullness. I have referred to Gershwin as ingenuous. This is a condescension with which articulate people often indulge themselves when speaking of the less articulate. There are moments when I gather that Gershwin is not unable to evaluate nicely his own place in society. He told me once that his mother had cautioned him against playing too much at parties. With engaging candor Gershwin admitted that there

217

might be some truth in this, but was it ingenuousness or sophistication which prompted him to add: "You see the trouble is, when I don't play, I don't have a good time!"?

1937·OLIN DOWNES

No other American composer had such a funeral service as that held last Thursday for George Gershwin. Not a MacDowell, not a Chadwick, not a Stephen Foster or Dan Emmett or John Philip Sousa received such parting honors. Authors, editors, playwrights and critics; national figures of the stage, the screen, the radio, the ballet; celebrated musicians, from Paul Whiteman to Walter Damrosch, composers as well as executants, gathered to say hail and farewell. This was eloquent of the place Gershwin held in the public esteem.

His immense success was due to his own great and indisputable talent and also to the period in American music. Some could read in this success and in the popular support of Gershwin a significant sign of the times. Popularly speaking, at least, Gershwin was the musical man of the hour. His rise to fortune was a Horatio Alger epic of Grand Street. As a boy he lived, played, fought, rose from poverty via the coop of a song-plugger in a music shop to the rank and fortune of the most widely known American composer. In that capacity, at the height of his reputation, he was busily producing, at one and the same time, light operas and orchestral works bid for by famous symphonic organizations. He was a public figure on two sides of the water, and all the concomitants of spectacular success were his.

He also benefited by the fact that metropolitan society was changing its ways, as, indeed, our ideas and manners were changing, the while that the conditions of urban life replaced the prevalently agricultural environment of the American of the former century. The day that saw a singing waiter make millions in music and eventually wed the daughter of a millionaire saw also the metamorphosis of the boy of immigrant parentage into a cosmopolite, who was sought by managers, interviewers, photographers, impresarios — yes, and young women of Park Avenue, who languished and leaned over the piano as George played. All this, and much more, happened to him, in the Babylonic epoch when everybody was so gay and everything so flush and amusing. He relished it, too, in an unbelievably naïve and simple way!

Gershwin had precisely the gift to delight and entertain. He was a born melodist, with a native instinct for exotic harmonic effects and the rhythmical ingenuity that usually pertain to musicians of his experience and kind. His way of playing the piano was maddeningly his own. He could never write down his accompaniments as he played them, although the edition of selected songs which appeared some six years ago had affixed to them a series of laughably appropriate embroideries on the melody for the keyed instrument. How original, felicitous and piquant were the best of the songs! How he could hit off a verse, preferably by his brother Ira! *Swanee, Stairway to Paradise, Sentimental Oriental Gentlemen Are We, Virginia, Lady Be Good* — these were inimitable miniatures. It need not be claimed that George had studied the laws of prosody with a scholar's passion. No. But he had the feeling of words, as the vaudevillian values them, and his musical style was the one tonal investiture for Ira's texts.

There is no need now to expatiate upon the details of the *Rhapsody in Blue,* but its consequences were many. One of them, which may not have worked out for the composer's best good, was that well-meaning critics and musical friends talked earnestly with George, and found him more than willing to attempt serious, even symphonic composition. He had shown that he could write a theme susceptible of symphonic treatment, granting that he could summon the necessary technic and structural power —a thing that he was not completely able to do. At the same time, he had shown dazzling possibilities in a new and original treatment of the outworn form of the piano concerto.

It is said that when Gershwin accepted the order of Damrosch and the New York Symphony to write a concerto in three movements he went out and bought a text book to find out what a concerto was! He made an astonishingly good attempt at the big form. It is a technical growth, but not a creative evolution. Essentially Gershwin sang one song. It is of the city, the music hall, the mechanical age. Granted poetry in the concerto's slow movement: it is the peace of the twilight outside the stage door. The doorkeeper puffs his cigar in the hot Summer evening, he sees blue and yellow electric lights, hears the echoes of the street, and the hum of the approaching elevated. It is city music, topical music, free of introspection or problems, written in a gay, thoughtless decade. It is sensuous, amorous and of a racy idiom, but it unfolds no broader horizon.

The best of the other orchestral works was undoubtedly *An American in Paris,* with the exhilarating hilarity of the "walking themes," and the unity of the impression augmented by amusing and personally devised instrumentation. The composition gets no farther than the earlier works; it reveals no new artistic or emotional ground. Gershwin strove in certain compositions toward the higher realms of composition. He looked into the promised land, and pointed a way—one way—that a greater musician might follow.

As it was, he displayed the immense virtues of his defects as a crafts-

221

man, his lack of musical background, his youthful ignorance of symphonic usage and tradition, and the environment which fortunately was not that of a standardized institution of musical learning, following with comfortable routine the century-old traditions of other lands and peoples than ours. Gershwin was free of that. He talked, musically speaking, the language that his countrymen and generation knew.

This, admittedly, was a dialect used by the less cultured of the populace, but it was a patois that every one understood, and one upon which a creative artist could genuinely build. Gershwin used the idiom in his own way. Others, such as Henry F. Gilbert and John Alden Carpenter, had approached the same issue through the medium of grander forms and complicated style. They were not widely understood. Gershwin was far enough from the bottom and near to the top to foreshadow an art that will spring from the people and sublimate their expression, but in a way that reflects the individuality of the thinker and artist.

No doubt Gershwin was materially aided in his career by the intense desire of his countrymen to see something of that sort happen in the development of an American music. It is also to be remembered that at least until the turn of the century few Americans took the study or cultivation of good music seriously. The man in the street passed Carnegie Hall distrustfully. A chap that composed was likely to be a "high-brow" or sissified, or both. The general popular acceptance, and indeed astonishing enthusiasm for great music by Bach and Wagner and Debussy and Strauss, to say nothing of a Bloch or Sibelius or Strawinsky, is a very recent thing. It was only in Gershwin's generation that the American people as a whole took with ardor to good music. He came on the scene just at the time to be a connecting link between the "serious" and "popular" composers of America. It was a highly desirable development.

And here is a point for consideration: the process, too often imitative, with our schooled composers, of imitating foreign models, versus another process, which is one of normal growth through creative energy and power of assimilation, on the part of our most gifted composers of light music. The conservatory student kneels before Mozart, Beethoven, Brahms, Wagner, Schumann or Strauss and it will be hard, indeed, for him to proceed in his work independently of these models.

But the man in Tin Pan Alley, of meager technical knowledge at best, writes the melody that comes into his head, writes to please. While he is doing that there comes into his ear a chord he has heard in a work by a classic master, and he finds he can profitably incorporate that progression in one of his songs. He does not imitate, he absorbs. The chances are all for the composer who grows upward rather than for the gentleman who condescendingly holds out a hand to people outside his circle, and who seems to fear anything savoring of common expressions. But they are good for native art. Doubtless the author of the *Rhapsody in Blue* was overrated, just as he and his ilk had in preceding days been grossly and snobbishly undervalued. It may soberly be said that the *Rhapsody in Blue* has had a strong and lasting influence for the good upon American composers.

They do tell the very amusing story, which can perfectly well be true, of Gershwin's asking Strawinsky to teach him composition, whereat Strawinsky is supposed to have asked, blandly, "What is your income per year?" When Gershwin, somewhat embarrassed, said he supposed it was in the neighborhood of $100,000 per annum, Strawinsky said, "Then I think you'd better teach me composition!" We shall certainly expose ourselves to contumely when we say that we would prefer one of the representative Gershwin's songs to many of the later compositions of Igor

223

Strawinsky. This despite the fact that Strawinsky almost invariably succeeds in putting down on paper what he wants there, thus carrying out to the last tone his musical conception. Gershwin could not do this, perhaps could not even harbor a conception that would require vast skill to realize. It remains that, as Debussy said, there is one music, which may inhabit a waltz or a symphony. Gershwin was en rapport much of the time, and in his own way, with that magic. Sometimes he conveyed it in a way that made him a pioneer of importance. This writer finds his expression limited, emotionally, imaginatively, stylistically. It is fundamentally popular music, jazz music and music which has intrigued the whole world. This writer has had jazz scraped and blared into his face in Tiflis. It is a music of a new color and it has given to the art new energy. Its elementary structures of jazz, its banalities, its defects in any amount you please, do not stultify its vitality and its wide appeal. It gained a new consideration with Gershwin, and Gershwin, in turn, contributed individual genius to the form. When the tumult and shouting are over—and already they are subsiding—he will have a secure place in the American tonal art.

George Gershwin

1933·GEORGE GERSHWIN

Unquestionably modern musical America has been influenced by modern musical Europe. But it seems to me that modern European composers, in turn, have very largely received their stimulus, their rhythms and impulses from Machine Age America. They have a much older tradition of musical technique which has helped them put into musical terms a little more clearly the thoughts that originated here. They can express themselves more glibly.

The Machine Age has influenced practically everything. I do not mean only music but everything from the arts to finance. The machine has not affected our age in form as much as in tempo, speed and sound. It has affected us in sound whenever composers utilize new instruments to imitate its aspects. In my *American in Paris* I used four taxi horns for musical effect. George Antheil has used everything, including aeroplane propellers, door bells, typewriter keys, and so forth. By the use of the old instruments, too, we are able to obtain modern effects. Take a composition like Honegger's *Pacific No. 231*, written and dedicated to a steam engine. It reproduces the whole effect of a train stopping and starting and it is all done with familiar instruments.

There is only one important thing in music and that is ideas and feeling. The various tonalities and sounds mean nothing unless they grow out of ideas. Not many composers have ideas. Far more of them know how to use strange instruments which do not require ideas. Whoever has inspired ideas will write the great music of our period. We are plowing the ground for that genius who may be alive or may be born today or tomorrow. If he is alive, he is recognized to a certain degree, although it is impossible for the public at large to assimilate real greatness quickly. Take a composer like Bach. In his lifetime, he was recognized as one of the greatest organists in the world, but he was not acclaimed as one of the greatest composers of his time or of all time until generations after his death.

I do not think there is any such thing as mechanized musical composition without feeling, without emotion. Music is one of the arts which appeals directly through the emotions. Mechanism and feeling will have to go hand in hand, in the same way that a skyscraper is at the same time a triumph of the machine and a tremendous emotional experience, almost breath-taking. Not merely its height but its mass and proportions are the result of an emotion, as well as of calculation.

Any discussion of the distinction between presentation and representation in music resolves itself into an attempt to determine the relative values of abstract music and program music. It is very difficult for anyone to tell where abstract music starts and program music finishes. There must have been a picture of something in the composer's mind. What it was nobody knows, often not even the composer. But music has a marvelous faculty of recording a picture in someone else's mind. In my own case, everybody who has ever listened to *Rhapsody in Blue*—and that embraces thousands of people—has a story for it but myself. *An American in Paris* is obviously a program piece, although I would say half of it or more is abstract music tied together by a few representative themes. Imitation never gets anyone anywhere. Originality is the only thing that counts. But

226

the originator uses material and ideas that occur around him and pass through him. And out of his experience comes this original creation or work of art, unquestionably influenced by his surroundings which include very largely what we call the Machine Age.

It is difficult to determine what enduring values, esthetically, jazz has contributed, because jazz is a word which has been used for at least five or six different types of music. It is really a conglomeration of many things. It has a little bit of ragtime, the blues, classicism and spirituals. Basically, it is a matter of rhythm. After rhythm in importance come intervals, music intervals which are peculiar to the rhythm. After all, there is nothing new in music. I maintained years ago that there is very little difference in the music of different nations. There is just that little individual touch. One country may prefer a peculiar rhythm or a note like the seventh. This it stresses, and it becomes identified with that nation. In America this preferred rhythm is called jazz. Jazz is music; it used the same notes that Bach used. When jazz is played in another nation, it is called American. When it is played in another country, it sounds false. Jazz is the result of the energy stored up in America. It is a very energetic kind of music, noisy, boisterous and even vulgar. One thing is certain. Jazz has contributed an enduring value to America in the sense that it has expressed ourselves. It is an original American achievement which will endure, not as jazz perhaps, but which will leave its mark on future music in one form or another. The only kinds of music which endure are those which possess form in the universal sense and folk music. All else dies. But unquestionably folk songs are being written and have been written which contain enduring elements of jazz. To be sure, that is only an element; it is not the whole. An entire composition written in jazz could not live.

227

As for further esthetic developments in musical composition, American composers may in time use quarter notes, but then so will Europe use quarter notes. Eventually our ears will become sensitive to a much finer degree than they were a hundred, fifty or twenty-five years ago. Music deemed ugly then is accepted without question today. It stands to reason, therefore, that composers will continue to alter their language. That might lead to anything. They have been writing already in two keys. There is no reason why they will not go further and ask us to recognize quarter or sixteenth notes. Such notes, whether written or not, are used all the time, only we are not conscious of them. In India they use quarter tones and, I believe, consciously.

Music is a phenomenon that to me has a very marked effect on the emotions. It can have various effects. It has the power of moving people to all of the various moods. Through the emotions, it can have a cleansing effect on the mind, a disturbing effect, a drowsy effect, an exciting effect. I do not know to what extent it can finally become a part of the people. I do not think music as we know it now is indispensable although we have music all around us in some form or other. There is music in the wind. People can live more or less satisfactorily without orchestral music, for instance. And who can tell that we would not be better off if we weren't as civilized as we are, if we lacked many of our emotions? But we have them and we are more or less egotistic about them. We think that they are important and that they make us what we are. We think that we are an improvement over people of other ages who didn't have them. Music has become a very important part of civilization, and one of the main reasons is that one does not need a formal education to appreciate it. Music can be appreciated by a person who can neither read nor write and it can also be appreciated by people who have the highest form of intelligence. For example, Einstein plays the violin and listens to music. People in the underworld, dope fiends and gun men, invariably are music lovers and, if not, they are affected by it. Music is entering into medicine. Music sets up a certain vibration which unquestionably results in a physical reaction. Eventually the proper vibration for every person will be found and utilized. I like to think of music as an emotional science.

Almost every great composer profoundly influences the age in which he lives. Bach, Beethoven, Wagner, Brahms, Debussy, Strawinsky. They have all recreated something of their time so that millions of people could feel it more forcefully and better understand their time.

The composer, in my estimation, has been helped a great deal by the mechanical reproduction of music. Music is written to be heard, and any instrument that tends to help it to be heard more frequently and by greater numbers is advantageous to the person who writes it. Aside from royalties or anything like that, I should think that the theory that music is written to be heard is a good one. To enable millions of people to listen to music by radio or phonograph is helpful to the composer. The composer who writes music for himself and doesn't want it to be heard is generally a bad composer. The first incursion of mechanized reproduction was a stimulus to the composer and the second wave has merely intensified that stimulus. In the past, composers have starved because of lack of performance, lack of being heard. That is impossible today. Schubert could not make any money because he did not have an opportunity through the means of distribution of his day to reach the public. He died at the age of thirty-one and had a certain reputation. If he had lived to be fifty or sixty, unquestionably he would have obtained recognition in his own day. If he were living today, he would be well-off and comfortable.

The radio and the phonograph are harmful to the extent that they bastardize music and give currency to a lot of cheap things. They are not harmful to the composer. The more people listen to music, the more they will be able to criticize it and know when it is good. When we speak of machine-made music, however, we are not speaking of music in the highest sense, because, no matter how much the world becomes a Machine Age, music will have to be created in the same old way. The Machine Age can affect music only in its distribution. Composers must compose in the same way the old composers did. No one has found a new method in which to write music. We still use the old signatures, the old symbols. The composer has to do every bit of his work himself. Hand work can never be replaced in the composition of music. If music ever became machine-made in that sense, it would cease to be an art.

BEVERLEY
1927·NICHOLS

I am going to begin right in the middle, because until I have made George Gershwin play you his first piano concerto you will probably regard him (as do most of our half-baked critics) as a mere pedlar of common tunes, like his *Swanee,* and *Lady, Be Good.* So you must imagine a swarthy young man of twenty-seven, seated at a piano by the open window of a room in Pall Mall not long ago, lifting his fingers and beginning to play. The twilight was fast fading when he sat down, and by the time he had finished it was almost dark, and the street lamps were lit. Yet in that brief period I had passed through one of the most singular musical experiences I have known.

I ought to be slightly drunk to be able to describe it properly, for it was the music of intoxication. Only by ragged words, by a mass of stage effects, by strident and jagged adjectives could one hope to recapture on the printed page the entangled and enticing rhythms which floated across the darkening room.

How can I describe those rhythms? Everybody is acquainted, of course, with the ordinary jazz tricks. Most of them consist in making a tune hiccup, by a judicious administration of quavers at the beginning of a bar. Or else, a simple phrase of six quavers, demanding a three-four tempo, is put into a strait-waistcoat of common time, and made to wriggle about with most entertaining antics. Everybody knows these little devices. They are as old as Bach, and probably older.

I realized in the first five minutes that Gershwin was going far beyond that in his concerto. It would need a very complicated series of mathematical charts to explain exactly what he *was* doing; and even when one had explained it, the number of people who could play the result would, I imagine, be not greater than those who, according to Mr. Einstein, comprehended the theory of relativity. To put it in a non-technical way, he was taking a quantity of strictly opposed rhythms and, by some magic counterpoint of his own, weaving them into a glittering mass which was at once as well ordered as a route march and as drunken as an orgy.

Yet beautiful. *Really* beautiful. The visions that this concerto called up before me! I loathe people who make pictures out of music, who grin vacuously and refer to waterfalls when they hear a Liszt cadenza, who poignantly recall their first seduction when listening to a sentimental waltz by Chaminade, and to whom the Preludes of Chopin mean nothing more than rain dripping on a roof or George Sand having the vapors. The world is full of such people, and I have always flattered myself that I was not of their number. Apparently I was mistaken.

For as I listened it seemed that the whole of new America was blossoming into beauty before me. The phrases swept up the piano with the stern, unfaltering grace of a skyscraper. Ever and anon the bass would take it into its head to go mad, with the fierce, orgiastic madness of a negro. There were passages vivid and humorous—a sort of chattering of Broadway chorus girls drinking mint julep at Child's. There were slow, secretive melodies that had in them something of the mystery of vast forests. The tunes clashed and fought, degenerated, were made clean again, joined together, and scampered madly over the keyboard in a final

232

rush which was as breathless as the thundering herd over the prairies of the West.

When it was all over, and the aftermath of silence had gradually been penetrated by the noises of everyday life from the streets outside, I felt that the occasion was one for repeating what Schumann said after hearing Chopin for the first time: "Hats off, gentlemen—a genius." Only there were no hats to take off, and we should both have been embarrassed by so un-English a display of emotion. I therefore turned to one of the most complicated pages and asked him, quite bluntly, how it was done.

"I don't know."

"Please play this bit very slowly."

He played it. There were three distinct rhythms fighting each other —two in the treble and one in the bass. I began to laugh.

"What are you laughing at?"

"All those rhythms—scrapping. How *do* you make them fight like that?"

He shook his head, and went on playing.

"I feel things inside, and then I work them out—that's all."

"You must have felt pretty volcanic when you wrote this. Do you always feel volcanic?"

"No. An ordinary jazz tune's different."

While he had been talking, he had been occasionally dabbing at the keyboard with his right hand. Little bits of tunes were born, floated away, died. Now and then he would play a phrase twice, three times, and then smother it with a discord, as though he did not wish to claim its paternity. Then, suddenly, a rather fascinating phrase came out.

233

"I say," I said, "I rather like that."

"So do I." He played it again, improvising a "following" theme. "It's got possibilities. But it's really a Charleston tune, and it hasn't got a Charleston rhythm." At which he proceeded to maltreat that poor tune as few tunes have been maltreated. Over and over again he played it, until I felt that I never wanted to hear it again. Then, when it seemed perfect, he said: "Well, at any rate, that's a beginning."

When I went to the first night of *Lady, Be Good* I heard the tune that had been begun that evening. You have probably heard it, too.

There—I am writing on silent paper, which has no power of harmony or discord, and I will cease from these descriptions of an art which cannot be described. But before I end, I want to tell what I should have told in the first few lines—how Gershwin, who has now an income much greater than the President of the United States, began. He said: "I began a few years ago in a little music-publishing house on Broadway. Every day at nine o'clock I was there at the piano, playing popular tunes for anybody who came along. Colored people used to come in and get me to play them *God Send You Back to Me* in seven keys. Chorus ladies used to breathe down my neck. Some of the customers treated one like dirt. Others were charming. Among the latter was Fred Astaire.

"It was at a time when Fred and Adele were doing a little vaudeville show of their own. Fred used to come in sometimes to hear the new songs. I remember saying to him once, 'Wouldn't it be wonderful if one day I could write a show of my own, and you and Adele could star in it?' We just laughed then. But it came true."

It certainly did.

234

NANETTE
1937·KUTNER

OUTSIDE

Uncle Dave said it. He said, "I'd rather own one rich relative who doesn't look at me than six poor ones who hang on my neck!"

Right after this, as if it were a sign, Minnie, our rich cousin, looked at us, indirectly of course, but she looked, reaching through the mails with a pair of tickets to a concert. "Perhaps you can use these," her secretary wrote.

Perhaps we could. At first we tried to give them away. Nobody wanted to go. The intellectuals scoffed at jazz. The others said they preferred The Palais Royal where you could *dance* to Paul Whiteman.

So we went, Uncle Dave who loves to get things for nothing, and I, who have no ear for music.

Sometime during the performance, it might have been towards the end of the first half, a man walked across the platform, and, even from where we were sitting, you could tell he was very young.

He paused at the piano which stood in the center. We heard a metallic clink, like the sound of a coin shooting through a slot. He smiled, sat down and gave an imitation of a player piano in a honky-tonk restaurant.

I don't remember whether the audience cared for this. More than likely they were surprised. I do remember his hurried walk, the long-legged hasty stride of one unaccustomed to parading in front of a crowd.

235

Later, probably near the end of the second half, Mr. Whiteman made an announcement. They would present, he said, a jazz composition which this young man had written for the occasion.

Then the orchestra played, accompanied by the composer, so new, so well-groomed, so politely seated at the piano.

I remember how that performance vested him with a kind of glamor. And I repeated his name. And the name of his piece. George Gershwin. The *Rhapsody in Blue.*

He must have gone abroad. At the early summer dress rehearsal of the *Scandals,* someone said he was in London. Bill Daly, co-worker, friend, conductor, could be seen the entire night, his skinny length stretching half out of the musicians' pit, his thick brown hair curling upright, scholarly spectacles planted upon his thin nose, while he stood, scribbled or waved his arms. No matter what he did, you noticed his back, an indomitable guardian, conscientiously bent over Gershwin's score.

Winnie Lightner came bouncing across a bare stage, orchid chiffon skirt swaying in the rhythm of the song she sang. The others, their exhausted bodies flung down in the vacant orchestra, as they waited through dreary pauses of a last rehearsal, these others were suddenly alert.

For the song did this to them, destined, by dint of its gusto, to be hummed, whistled, joyously carried from that tired workshop and sung in thousands of places in the days to come.

> *"Somebody loves me,
> I wonder who,
> I wonder who he can be."

---

* Copyright 1924 by Harms Inc.

But the show was too long. Something had to be cut. Out went *Congo Kate.*

A simple matter to kill a sketch, a costume or a set, a matter of discrimination, and if your money is invested, guts. Doing away with a song is something else. *Congo Kate,* pronounced finished, popped up for weeks, its foolish jingle persistent, running through our brains; its fuel replenished by a little girl, sitting cross-legged on the apron of an empty stage, her Dutch bobbed head leaning above a ukulele, her fingers plucking at its strings.

Rehearsal memories stamped forever, by Bill Daly peering at a score he loved, and the girl, Hannah Williams, hugging a banjo and singing a discarded song because she couldn't help it.

INSIDE

Meeting him proved a shock.

Here was no art pose, but a blatant earthiness. God be praised . . . he was alive; lusty, suntanned, athletic; wearing blue shirts, smoking black cigars.

Musically he could re-create the tempo of our day because he naturally spoke its crude cards-on-the-table lingo. *"Do, do, do, what you done, done, done before, baby." His flavor, accurately caught by one of brother Ira's lyrics.

We met in the white house on One Hundred-and-third Street, a neighborhood too far up and too far west to be rated good New York.

You rang the front door bell, a terrier yelped, a maid, neither prompt nor neat, answered, or his mother or his sister Frances. And you were shown to a small elevator. On the way, left of the entrance hall you saw

---

* Copyright 1926 by Harms Inc.

a mirrored room, its formal design routed by a ping-pong table; George's touch.

Mounting past numerous bedrooms, past a parlor with two pianos, you reached the top. This was his.

The front, a living-workroom, neat brick fireplace, grand piano, unassuming comfortable furniture, could have taken root anywhere. Its windows, half smothered by a stone-walled balcony, so you glimpsed only a roof and part of the sky, a cut-off view, remote, tucking the room out of the way, giving a sense of city.

In the back was a spacious bedroom; linked between, the small study, floor patterned in black-and-white checker-board squares, walls sliding paneled cupboards, built for manuscripts. About these he was enthusiastic, showing them off, along with the two autographed pictures framed above his desk...one of Charles Chaplin, the other, the face and signature of the Duke of Kent..."To George from George."

It was still new to him, celebrities, success. His rich voice excitedly described a party he had just given. "They had the run of the house. They did stunts! Everyone was here! Like Marc Connelly!"

He was busy with the *Oh, Kay* score. He had letters to write. And no one to write them. Autograph demands multiplied. The letters lay unanswered. It did not occur to him to have a secretary.

He finally purchased a portable typewriter, for a while playing with the keys, entranced.

Then we started on the letters. First, those in the chest of drawers near the bed. A note from Lady Diana Manners. One from Adele Astaire who puzzled him; her lovable outspoken breeziness remaining a mystery to his nature, self-conscious and studied.

With the autographs he was painstaking. To W. H. Handy went a copy of the *Rhapsody,* signed "For the Father Of The Blues."

Mornings, Bill Daly often present, he worked at the piano. As he played he sang wordless strains over and over again. He said, "I do it until I get it right."

He thought in a straight line, showing me a thin book, declaring, "Some day I'll make an opera out of it." The book, just published, was titled *Porgy.*

Pictures come forward, like quick shots on the screen. When, exuberant, he danced the "Black Bottom," to see if its steps fitted his rhythms; the time he argued, "But everybody's got an ear!" refusing to credit my inherent lack; the rainy afternoon he thought was "a swell day to work if I had an idea"; the morning his greeting exploded, "I woke up at three with a tune, even the title! I got right up and wrote it, like you read about! But now . . . it's not so hot!"

It wasn't. It was *I've Got Fidgety Feet,* one of the lesser lights in *Oh, Kay.*

At that time, of his own popular ones, his favorite, *I'll Build a Stairway to Paradise.*

The Man I Love had already been cut from the English *Lady, Be Good.* "Not a production number," he said.

And "Here's a song I want to be a sort of 'Long, Long Trail'." He shot wide of his mark, yet, of those who heard her sing it, who can forget Gertrude Lawrence's plaintive plea for *Someone to Watch Over Me.*

So he worked, in quiet, but for interruptions illuminating the family life buzzing below us. Once his sister hollered up the stairs, "I've got to have the money for my dancing lessons!" Once his brother Ira's fiancee reported on the patient's progress, Ira having lost an appendix.

239

And once the pictures came. The walls had been adorned with caricatures of composers, caricatures he liked to explain, delighted to share his new found knowledge. Now Mr. Beethoven and Brahms were tossed aside to make room for two prize-fight lithographs by Bellows. Work for the day stopped while, refusing assistance, he stood upon the sofa and hung those manly scenes himself.

Eager to help others, he was always recommending people. For his sister he wrote a note to George White, reading, "You gave the first Gershwin his chance, why not another?"

That year the *Scandals* utilized his *Rhapsody.* He asked nothing for this, yet was grateful when given an opening night box.

On his twenty-seventh birthday his photograph appeared in the New York Times. He telephoned, "You wouldn't believe it, but everyone saw that picture and congratulated me!"

The next summer he appeared with the Philharmonic Symphony Orchestra as soloist in an all Gershwin program at the Lewisohn Stadium, drawing a record crowd of about eighteen thousand listeners.

The following day I met him on the street. He was rushing from a rehearsal of *Strike Up The Band.*

He shouted, "Look what I've got here!" Pushing me into a cab, he dropped a pile of clippings on my lap. "The write-ups about last night!"

My mind wandered back to that scared young man at his first concert, then jumped to this one whom I had seen the night before, running down a flight of steps towards his audience, as if he was glad and couldn't wait to meet them.

He had come far in such a short time. He kept going too, the pulse of his career as fast as Colonel Lindbergh's airplane that had just flown

240

across the Atlantic, as fast as the taxi that was hurtling us up town or the radio waves that had already carried news of his success, news bubbling from his lips while he sat there, boyish, marveling at everything. And I held my breath and I hoped it would continue. His life was so wonderful.

He leased an apartment, glaringly modern, a penthouse on Riverside Drive, away from the bulk of his family. There was a silver piano, and a bedroom that seemed all bed, the cover of light tan fur. Nothing out of place here, a punching bag in the room meant for games, a man wearing a white coat, who answered the door.

He still ran to the telephone himself. Any summons could mean another miracle.

His moods changed. Losing his temper at Ira. "Why don't you attend to things for me!" Awed at the prospect of study with Ravel. Thirsty hero-worshipping of those who knew more musically than he, Ernest Newman, Strawinsky. Hurt surprise over a failure. Pacing the floor about it, shouting, *"They forget everything you've done when you make one mistake!"*

Incredulous anger at Ziegfeld who held back royalties because *Show Girl* wasn't a hit. Dignified, dependable, he expected others to be the same. George Gershwin was probably the only man on Broadway who didn't have a lawyer.

His discipline superb, he could not understand Vincent Youmans being side-tracked into producing plays. For he had one objective. Through the years his greeting to me, "Haven't you written your 'Rhapsody' yet?" revealed what that first ambitious work had grown to mean.

It was a treacherous light, dividing him, making him, now well-accustomed to privileges, drill at his gusher of popular tunes, while forcing a humble steady studying, a learning day by day, as he tried living up to an artistic dream created by adulation.

241

Thorough, he could not tolerate carelessness. Shaking his head, he told me of the night Rudy Vallee broadcast the *Concerto*. "We had to mark the pages so he could get the beats."

On his part he puzzled others. Vincent Youmans, one day his junior, grumbled, "Doesn't he know society only invites us if we bring along a piano!"

He knew, and relished that piano and the playing of his songs in the center of a smart crowd.

He was big enough to have dragged his family on, up with him, some of this good heartedness a sop to fate, a bargaining with a life that had generously catapulted him beyond his sphere.

He was not unique. Others traced that pattern. Who knows? In every profession, each, at the top, for all the hard work and God-given talents, might have been looking at his fellow men, not really believing he belonged, trying to out-do that last effort, dreading the one mistake, waiting for the day his gift would disappear as unreasonably as it came, each, a little boy, knowing rewards were out of proportion, feeling he didn't deserve quite so much, scared to death of his nightmare overtaking him.

He moved again to a duplex apartment on the east side. The enormous high-ceilinged living-room, fitting background for his newly acquired art collection, a modern and expensive assortment, wherein Gershwin's impression of his father audaciously stared at a Rosseau.

He loved that room. "Done by one of our best decorators," he said, oblivious to the naked shelves, deserted but for an occasional unread book.

He painted now. At one end of the dining room hung a self-portrait, the shade of the skin browner, the face longer, leaner than the model's. Upstairs, in an easel-scattered studio stood his proudest study,

242

a colored girl from Catfish Row. This second talent, amazing, not only for its own qualities, but because he made the time and found the energy to develop it.

He planned touring with an orchestra. At the end of rehearsals, as he stood upon the podium, his well-cut suit was a contrast to those baggy pants of the musicians who surrounded him.

They were leaving the next week.

"What do you want us to wear?" came the question.

The answer, his order, unhesitating, "Morning coats, pin striped trousers."

A silence then, broken by one speaking, low-toned, timid. "But I haven't got them."

He appeared surprised. He had forgotten that these men, fine musicians, went weeks, months, without work, that they continually faced the bread-robbing horror of mechanical sound. And he must have felt ashamed as he stood before them, so embarrassingly successful. For a look of compassion crossed his face. "Wear what you have," he said, his voice gentle.

He grew thoughtless. Once, after having me wait two hours, he walked into the dining room saying that I could watch him eat.

The following day he was sorry, running everywhere, showing me the new bar, the English den, the ink spattered studio on the second floor. He was the George who had joyously exhibited special cupboards in One Hundred-and-third Street; now it was a working desk he designed, and a humidor presented in honor of *An American in Paris,* engraved with names like Otto Kahn, Jules Glaenzer, Irving Berlin.

He was indignant when he heard people criticize him for allowing a cathartic company to be his radio sponsors. "They forget it gives me enough money to spend months on an opera."

Porgy and Bess was his triumph. No Ferde Grofé, no Bill Daly to help here. "Look," as he handed me the thick score. "I orchestrated the whole business . . . every note myself!"

Towards the cast he felt paternal, loving the fact that he selected them. "My Bubbles can dance rings around Astaire."

These days, a difference, he was very nervous. Glimpse of his old enthusiasm would shine through it all, but most of the time he seemed worried. "I can't sleep. I'm being psyched. I can't fall in love."

And I remember thinking that here was a man who didn't have much fun.

Then Winchell reported he was seriously ill. I read this aloud on the roof of a Broadway hotel, overheard by Frances Williams, the blues singer, by a crooner with Ben Bernie's band, a saxophonist who worked for Guy Lombardo.

In a night club Frances Williams had once sung a lyric to the *Rhapsody*. She said, "When he heard it, Gershwin kissed me."

Throwing back her blond head, she sang it again, shouted it to the smoky city skies, while the crooner and the saxophonist hummed a swinging accompaniment and from down below in the pit of the streets the variegated honks of traffic horns rose to join them.

As the melody floated off the roof, floated one block eastward to the Carnegie he loved so much, I could not help thinking that although Bill Daly, the faithful, had long since died, and little Hannah Williams was a matron named Mrs. Jack Dempsey, there would, no matter what happened, always be people to keep Gershwin's songs alive.

AFTER

I was wrong. I reckoned without death.

As long as the abrupt stopping of a life was news that could be tele-typed, printed, photographed, broadcast, they were interested, he could keep pace.

A radio concert the night after, time and distance shot. California, Fred Astaire speaks; Texas, Whiteman plays; we hear Jolson from New York.

In spite of the heat and the rain, the funeral, in the heavy, bronze-doored temple had standing room only. Thirty rows down front reserved for his family and for the first night, first rate elite, men-about-town, society, politics, the arts. "There's Bennett Cerf, Cobina Wright . . ." Necks stretched, heads turned, shoulders pushed, voices whispered, ris-ing, "There's the Mayor." "There's George M. Cohan." "There's Jimmy Walker!"

It seemed as if he were there, putting on another show, making his relatives proud of him.

In the back balcony, far from the reserved section, the man seated next to me smelled badly. He smelled from subway sweat, from Second Avenue, from the terrific distance he journeyed in all that heat. Whoever he was, butcher, barber, tailor, neighbor, he sobbed with a cry that had retched its way past throats of many cantors, echoing itself in the melodic wails of the boy he loved. For he must have loved him and the songs he made, this man with the gasping sobs, the wringing hands and the Hebrew paper, honest label, sticking from his pocket.

Dead. Stopped. Finished. Not so fast. True, the radio was tapering off, but the Stadium planned a concert. The rich were buying their tables two

245

weeks in advance; the poor carry their suppers as they wait; the ones who knew him can't believe, still hear his deep voice ringing in their ears.

An audience of twenty thousand, breaking his own record and that of Heifetz who played the week before. They keep on coming, crowding, shoving until the last seat is taken. Their felt hats, chalk white, pastels, dotting a summer-shaded climb, up and up, with here and there long legs dangling over, molding the circusy perspiring mass that seems to recede, lean back a bit, almost touch the clouded skies.

Stretching, whispering. "There's the Governor." "There's the Mayor." My cousin Minnie. "Ethel Merman's gonna sing." Cig-ar-ettes, coca-cola, pop, root beer.

With the first note a heavenly conductor plants a star. It twinkles high above a gothic tower. His songs begin.

Sweltering, they listen, attentive, sentimental for the moment. The second half, they rise in silent prayer. It's thrilling, doing what the Governor is doing, what the Mayor is doing, the thing to do.

Impressed, they sit again, but now it is as if a secret signal told each one the drama part was through, this man done for, a restlessness commences, a constant murmuring, a feeling of things over.

From the back. "Ethel Merman had fur on her dress." "Those colored singers sure were fine." "We'd better go, avoid the rush."

What matter the *Rhapsody* to be played, an eloquent finale, the *Rhapsody* that shaped his soul, his life and plans.

From the center. "You've heard the *Rhapsody* before . . . come on."

From a table. "I can't forget dear Gawge in London, his hair and shoes just too, too shiny. But my dear, where *did* you get that dress?"

This a Greek chorus up-to-date.

246

When the *Rhapsody* tears torrid atmosphere, the mass disintegrates without a beg-your-pardon. Snake-like it weaves its fickle way towards every exit, so as the last chord strikes they, who feel no honest love for gentleness, for peaceful void, will have no more. Steadfastness takes minute upon minute, days and years, is not for those who rush, not for the tough, the speedy, the live, well on their way to autos that can race them home, to subways that can travel faster.

Then I knew. We find no time for last month's death, nor for its after-math, the patient stationary quiet, no time to cry out, even to him who knew, feared, felt our modern hearts, pace-setting, whip-cracking.

So I pause, give credit, bow and say, "Oh, George, you made your one mistake! It was to die."

WORKS OF
GEORGE GERSHWIN

CONCERT WORKS

1923 135TH STREET. One-act opera; libretto by B. G. DeSylva ... 1924 RHAPSODY IN BLUE ... 1925 CONCERTO IN F ... 1926 PRELUDES ... 1928 AN AMERICAN IN PARIS ... 1931 SECOND RHAPSODY ... 1932 PIANO TRANSCRIPTION OF 18 SONGS. CUBAN OVERTURE ... 1934 VARIATIONS on I GOT RHYTHM ... 1935 GRAND OPERA—PORGY AND BESS. Libretto by DuBose Heyward. Lyrics by DuBose Heyward and Ira Gershwin.

FOR THE THEATRE

1919 .. LA LA LUCILLE; lyrics, B. G. DeSylva and Arthur Jackson; book, Frederick Jackson.

1920 .. THE MIDNIGHT WHIRL; lyrics, B. G. DeSylva; book, John Henry Mears.
GEORGE WHITE'S SCANDALS; lyrics, Arthur Jackson.

1921 .. A DANGEROUS MAID; lyrics, Ira Gershwin; book, Charles W. Bell.
GEORGE WHITE'S SCANDALS; lyrics, Arthur Jackson.

1922 .. GEORGE WHITE'S SCANDALS; lyrics, B. G. DeSylva and E. Ray Goetz.
OUR NELL; lyrics, Brian Hooker; book, A. E. Thomas.
(With William Daly)

1923 .. GEORGE WHITE'S SCANDALS; lyrics, B. G. DeSylva.
RAINBOW REVUE; lyrics, Clifford Grey; book, Edgar Wallace. (London)
SWEET LITTLE DEVIL; lyrics, B. G. DeSylva; book, Laurence Schwab and Frank Mandel. (London)

1924 .. PRIMROSE; lyrics, Ira Gershwin and Desmond Carter; book, Guy Bolton and Fred Thompson. (London)
STOP FLIRTING; lyrics, Ira Gershwin and Arthur Jackson; book, Frederick Jackson and Fred Thompson. (London—with Paul Lannin and William Daly.)
LADY BE GOOD; lyrics, Ira Gershwin; book, Guy Bolton and Fred Thompson.
GEORGE WHITE'S SCANDALS; lyrics, B. G. DeSylva and Ballard McDonald.

248

1925 .. TELL ME MORE; lyrics, B. G. DeSylva and Ira Gershwin; book, Fred Thompson and Wm. K. Wells.
TIP TOES; lyrics, Ira Gershwin; book, Guy Bolton and Fred Thompson.
SONG OF THE FLAME; lyrics, Oscar Hammerstein II; book, Otto Harbach. (With Herbert Stothart)

1926 .. OH, KAY; lyrics, Ira Gershwin; book, P. G. Wodehouse and Guy Bolton.

1927 .. FUNNY FACE; lyrics, Ira Gershwin; book, Fred Thompson and Paul Gerard Smith.
STRIKE UP THE BAND; lyrics, Ira Gershwin; book, Geo. S. Kaufman.
ROSALIE; lyrics, P. G. Wodehouse and Ira Gershwin; book, Guy Bolton and Wm. Anthony McGuire. (With Sigmund Romberg)

1928 .. TREASURE GIRL; lyrics, Ira Gershwin; book, Vincent Laurence and Fred Thompson.

1929 .. SHOW GIRL; lyrics, Ira Gershwin and Gus Kahn; book, Wm. Anthony McGuire.
STRIKE UP THE BAND; lyrics, Ira Gershwin; book, Morrie Ryskind and Geo. S. Kaufman. (Revised Edition)

1930 .. GIRL CRAZY; lyrics, Ira Gershwin; book, Guy Bolton and Jack McGowan.

1931 .. DELICIOUS; lyrics, Ira Gershwin; book, Guy Bolton and Sonya Levien. (Film)
OF THEE I SING; lyrics, Ira Gershwin; book, Geo. S. Kaufman and Morrie Ryskind. (Pulitzer Prize Winner)

1932 .. PARDON MY ENGLISH; lyrics, Ira Gershwin; book, Herbert Fields and Jack McGowan.

1933 .. LET 'EM EAT CAKE; lyrics, Ira Gershwin; book, Geo. S. Kaufman and Morrie Ryskind.

1937 .. SHALL WE DANCE; lyrics, Ira Gershwin; book, Allan Scott and E. Pogano. (Film)
A DAMSEL IN DISTRESS; lyrics, Ira Gershwin; book, P. G. Wodehouse, S. K. Lauren and E. Pogano. (Film)
GOLDWYN FOLLIES; lyrics, Ira Gershwin; book, Ben Hecht. (Film)

ALSO CONTRIBUTED
SONGS TO THE FOLLOWING SHOWS

1918 .. HALF PAST EIGHT, LOOK WHO'S HERE; 1919 .. BROADWAY BREVITIES, DERE MABLE; 1920 .. SWEETHEART SHOP, GOOD MORNING JUDGE, SINBAD, THE LADY IN RED, BLUE EYES; 1922 .. THE FRENCH DOLL, THE NIFTIES; 1923 .. LITTLE MISS BLUEBEARD; 1924 .. AMERICANA.

VICTOR (RCA) RECORDS

AN AMERICAN IN PARIS (Gershwin) Parts 1 and 2. George Gershwin-Victor Symphony Orchestra. No. 35963.

AN AMERICAN IN PARIS (Gershwin) Parts 3 and 4. George Gershwin-Victor Symphony Orchestra. No. 35964.

PORGY AND BESS (Heyward-Gershwin). Tibbett-Jepson-Cho. and Orchestra. Album C-25 (11878-11881). *It Ain't Necessarily So*—F. T.— and *I Got Plenty o' Nuttin'*—F. T.—Lombardo's Royal Canadians. No. 25204.

RHAPSODY IN BLUE (Gershwin). By Boston "Pops" Orchestra, conducted by Arthur Fiedler. Album M-358 (11822-11823).
By Whiteman's Concert Orchestra, and Part 2—Whiteman's Concert Orchestra. No. 35822.
By Jesse Crawford, Organ, and Part 2—Crawford. No. 22343.
By Eight Piano Ensemble, and Part 2—Eight Piano Ensemble. No. 36123.

STRIKE UP THE BAND (Gershwin). Boston "Pops" Orchestra. *Rhapsody in Blue* —Part 3 (Inc. in M-358). Boston "Pops" Orchestra. No. 11823.

COLUMBIA RECORDS

CONCERTO IN F, for piano and orchestra; six parts. Roy Bargy, Whiteman and orchestra. Set No. 280.

MEMORIES: *Lady Be Good, I'll Build a Stairway to Paradise, The Man I Love, S' Wonderful, I Got Rhythm, Rhapsody in Blue.* Savoy Hotel Orpheans. (Kern Medley). No.7346-M.

LET'S CALL THE WHOLE THING OFF (from the film "Shall We Dance"). Hildegarde and Gibbon's Orchestra. (They Can't). No. 296-M.

PRELUDES NOS. 1 AND 2, George Gershwin (piano). No. 7192-M.

PRELUDE NO. 3; ANDANTE (from *Rhapsody in Blue*). George Gershwin (piano). No. 7192-M.

THEY CAN'T TAKE THAT AWAY FROM ME (from the film "Shall We Dance"). Hildegarde and Gibbon's Orchestra. (Let's Call). No. 296-M.

ACKNOWLEDGMENTS

Acknowledgment is made to the following individuals and publications for permission to reprint materials listed below:

George Gershwin and American Youth, An Appreciation . . Otto H. Kahn
    Musical Courier, January 22, 1929.

The Composer in the Machine Age . . . . George Gershwin
    Reprinted from *Revolt in the Arts,* edited by Oliver M. Saylor.
    Copyright, 1933, by Coward-McCann, Inc.

Rhapsody in Catfish Row . . . . George Gershwin
    New York Times, Sunday, October 20, 1935.

Hail and Farewell . . . . Olin Downes
    New York Times, July 18, 1937.

George Gershwin As Orchestrator . . . . William Daly
    New York Times, January 15, 1933.

George Gershwin . . . . Beverley Nichols
    Reprinted from *Are They The Same At Home?*
    Copyright, 1927, by Doubleday, Doran and Company.

The Gershwin Case . . . . Gilbert Seldes
    Esquire, October, 1934.

To George Gershwin . . . . Oscar Hammerstein II
    The George Gershwin Memorial Concert Programme,
    Hollywood Bowl, September 8, 1937.

Porgy and Bess Return On Wings of Song . . . . . . DuBose Heyward
    Stage Magazine, October, 1935.

Portrait In Our Time . . . . Nanette Kutner
    Copyright, February, 1938, by Esquire-Coronet Inc.

George Gershwin, A Lament . . . . Erma Taylor
    Jones' Magazine, November, 1937.

Profile . . . . S. N. Behrman
    The New Yorker, May 25, 1929.

ACKNOWLEDGMENTS

The preface by Merle Armitage, and the articles by Paul Whiteman, Walter Damrosch, Ferde Grofé, Arnold Schoenberg, Jerome Kern, Louis Danz, George Antheil, Merle Armitage, Serge Koussevitzky, Eva Gauthier, Irving Berlin, Albert Heink Sendrey, Leonard Liebling, Isamu Noguchi, Rudy Vallee, Lester Donahue, Sam H. Harris, Harold Arlen, Alexander Steinert, J. Rosamond Johnson, Isaac Goldberg, Henry A. Botkin, David Ewen, Todd Duncan, Ira Gershwin, and Rouben Mamoulian, were written especially for this book.

Reproduction of painting by Alfaro Siqueiros used on Title Page.

Carlos Dyer made the two end-paper ink-drawings for this volume.

The Covarrubias caricature of George Gershwin, copyright, 1925, *Vanity Fair,* reprinted by special permission of The Condé Nast Publications, Inc.

Caricature of George Gershwin by Peggy Bacon, from *Off With Their Heads,* copyright by McBride.

Hand lettering on Title Page by Wm. Stutz.

Reproductions of George Gershwin paintings printed by permission of The Gershwin Family.

Photographs by Otto Rothschild, Maurice Goldberg, Crown Features, RKO Radio Pictures, Inc., Pinchot, Keystone, Rex Hardy Jr., Time, Inc.

The list of George Gershwin's compositions was provided by Ira Gershwin.

Ramiel McGehee has contributed valuable assistance in research and revision.